Teacher
Self-Evaluation
Tool Kit

Teacher
Self-Evaluation
Tool Kit

Peter W. Airasian
Arlen R. Gullickson

CORWIN PRESS, INC.
A Sage Publications Company
Thousand Oaks, California

For information address:

 Corwin Press, Inc.
A Sage Publications Company
2455 Teller Road
Thousand Oaks, California 91320
e-mail: order@corwin.sagepub.com

SAGE Publications Ltd.
6 Bonhill Street
London EC2A 4PU
United Kingdom

SAGE Publications India Pvt. Ltd.
M-32 Market
Greater Kailash I
New Delhi 110 048 India

Printed in the United States of America

Library of Congress Cataloging-in-Publication Data

Airasian, Peter W.
    Teacher self-evaluation tool kit / Peter W. Airasian, Arlen R.
Gullickson.
        p.   cm.
    Includes bibliographical references.
    ISBN 0-8039-6516-8 (acid-free paper). — ISBN
0-8039-6517-6 (pbk. : acid-free paper)
    A. Teachers—Self-rating of—United States.   I. Gullickson, Arlen
R.   II. Title.
    LB2838.A37   1996
    371.1'44—dc20   96-25387

This book is printed on acid-free paper.

97 98 99 00 01 10 9 8 7 6 5 4 3 2

Corwin Press Production Editor: S. Marlene Head
Typesetter: Rebecca Evans
Cover Designer: Marcia R. Finlayson

Contents

Foreword

The effective teacher is among America's most important resources, and teaching is a profound professional responsibility. The effective teacher ignites enthusiasm, responsibility, curiosity, and creativity in students and guides them to become accomplished, self-directed learners and productive citizens. Ineffective teachers do great harm to students, families, and the society; they turn off students, misdirect them, and deter them from fulfilling their potential to become self-actualizing, informed, productive citizens. Families, government, business and industry, and other societal groups have a large stake in assuring that schools employ competent, effective teachers. Under poor teaching, student development suffers, and schools with poor teachers put the nation at risk, morally, socially, and economically. However, well-educated students will strengthen the nation's social well-being and economic competitiveness.

It is imperative, therefore, that schools effectively evaluate teachers. Schools need teacher evaluation to assist every teacher to assess and improve performance and to ensure they hire and retain only competent teachers. Teachers themselves are responsible, as are all professionals, for contributing to the evaluation of their work. Teacher self-evaluation has become especially important in light of recent trends toward making teachers more responsible and accountable for student outcomes and for their own professional development.

Among other evaluation responsibilities, teachers must regularly examine the needs and progress of their students; assess the effectiveness of teaching methods, materials, and activities; examine their success in partnering with other professionals and parents; and review the adequacy and currency of their content knowledge and teaching skills. Sound self-evaluation provides essential cues and leads to the improvement of one's teaching. It gives feedback on the success of teaching-improvement efforts, keeps teachers ready to issue needed accountability reports, and guides their professional growth. It also helps teachers experience the joy of knowing they are continually improving in their important job of educating students.

However, self-evaluation is often suspect. It can lack perspective and depth and be biased, heavily self-serving, or not convincing to parents and other stakeholders. Although sound self-evaluation is important, poor practice of it can misinform, mislead, impair credibility, and result in poor teaching. Schools need sound guidelines and defensible tools and strategies to overcome the threats to effective teacher self-evaluation.

Teacher Self-Evaluation Tool Kit is a valuable resource to help teachers employ rigorous guidelines and tools to evaluate their competence and performance. It includes a diverse and well-organized set of evaluation forms, guidelines, and procedures that are based on a sound concept of evaluation and how it relates to the improvement of instruction and teacher accountability. The authors define teacher self-evaluation as "a process in which teachers make judgments about the adequacy and effectiveness of their own knowledge, performance, beliefs, or effects for the purpose of self-improvement." The contents of the book cover the planning, implementation, reporting, and use of self-evaluation. This book should help both school principals and teachers increase and improve instruction and accountability through the sound practice of self-evaluation.

Teacher Self-Evaluation Tool Kit is well grounded in scholarly inquiry and practical experience. Its authors, Peter Airasian and Arlen Gullickson, are acknowledged experts in teacher self-evaluation, the broader area of personnel evaluation, and reflective teaching. They provide many practical examples and offer cogent advice on using the book.

Ultimate beneficiaries of this book will be students. In making effective use of it, the teacher will examine student needs; assure that instructional plans are keyed to meeting the needs of all the students; look critically at the effectiveness of teaching activities in addressing student needs; obtain pertinent feedback on teaching from students, parents, and peers; assess student progress; report to students and parents; and continuously review and improve the overall instructional process. Schools and teachers will find the this book a valuable resource for professionalizing and improving teaching.

DANIEL L. STUFFLEBEAM
The Evaluation Center
Western Michigan University

Preface

Evaluation of teaching is an essential aspect of teacher improvement. Teacher evaluation is required in virtually all U.S. schools as a means to ensure teacher accountability and improve teaching. Yet teacher evaluation has been regularly and appropriately criticized as being improperly conducted and ineffective in promoting teacher development. In 1990, calls for improvement of teacher evaluation made their way to Washington, D.C., where the U.S. Congress called for study and improvement of teacher evaluation practices. In response, the U.S. Department of Education awarded The Evaluation Center at Western Michigan University a 5-year grant to conduct research on ways to improve teacher evaluation and to disseminate findings and products to U.S. school districts. The research and development center was named the Center for Research on Educational Accountability and Teacher Evaluation (CREATE). CREATE's main purposes were to explore means to

- Validly and reliably evaluate teacher, administrator, and institutional performance
- Effectively use evaluation results to improve educational services to students and communities
- Credibly and systematically assure accountability to constituents and sponsors

Though most of CREATE's work focused on formal, external evaluations of teachers, primarily for accountability purposes, several CREATE projects focused on the problem of linking teacher evaluation to the professional development needs of teachers. This book is the result of a CREATE project that focused specifically on teacher evaluation for professional growth and development. That project's two aims were to

1. Enhance understanding of the role that teacher self-evaluation plays in elementary and secondary classrooms
2. Provide new or expanded options for teachers to use to enhance their knowledge and teaching skills

Preliminary steps in developing this book were based on a review of current teacher evaluation literature and focus-group interviews with teachers in six states. That development work, summarized in *Teacher Self-Evaluation: The Literature in Perspective*, helped us in a variety of ways. It provided substantial insight into teacher perspectives on self-evaluation, traditional principal evaluation, and professional development. It helped us clarify the role and potential of teacher self-evaluation. It established that although formal self-evaluation methods are advocated as a strong teacher development tool, they are used infrequently by teachers. It identified several major problems and barriers to teacher self-evaluation. It provided many useful examples of teacher self-evaluation strategies and recommendations for improving the self-evaluation process. It showed clearly why teacher self-evaluations often fail to meet standards of accepted evaluation standards. Importantly, our review revealed that instruction on how to conduct teacher self-evaluations is not a part of current practice for either preservice teachers or practicing teachers.

Teacher Self-Evaluation Tool Kit draws on these findings and provides what we believe are effective steps to help teachers conduct high-quality and useful self-evaluations. The book distinguishes teacher self-evaluation from other types of evaluation activities that teachers engage in, explains the importance of teacher self-evaluation, provides tools (strategies) that teachers can use to carry out self-evaluation, and, perhaps most important, provides direction to teachers and administrators on the proper conditions for initiating and maintaining teacher self-evaluation. We believe those who follow our guidance will profit from their self-evaluation efforts and find that they effectively serve teacher development needs. The book is intended to be a self-help resource for teachers who want to engage in self-evaluation and as an aid for the preservice and inservice instruction of teachers. Although this book is specifically intended for teachers, we think self-evaluation can be a strong tool for administrators who want to both assist teachers in their quest for professional development and carry out their own self-evaluations.

The information and strategies provided here are intended as beginning points. Much work remains for teacher self-evaluation to achieve its potential in helping teachers improve their knowledge and skills. We have pro-

vided the basics for helping teachers and administrators begin to understand the role of self-evaluation and conduct their own self-evaluations. We
expect that the creativity and insight of teachers and administrators will
carry our thoughts and suggestions well beyond the contents of this book as
teachers, schools, and districts apply self-evaluation in their own unique
contexts.

Acknowledgments

We are indebted to many people for their timely encouragement, support,
assistance, and critical comments. Our thanks to Dr. Daniel Stufflebeam,
who provided us the opportunity to propose and conduct this study under
the auspices of the CREATE grant and for his advice and guidance during
the conducting of our work; to the U.S. Department of Education's Office of
Educational Research and Improvement (OERI) for directly funding our research work; to our graduate assistants, Ms. Lisa Hahn (Western Michigan
University) and Ms. Ann Jones (Boston College), who played important
roles in conducting the literature review and focus-group interviews; to Dr.
Judy Burry-Stock (University of Alabama–Tuscaloosa) and Mr. Dale Farland
(University of South Dakota), who conducted focus-group interviews; to the
large array of teachers who took personal time to provide us with their in-
sights, perspectives, and descriptions of practice; to Dr. Paula Egelson and
Dr. Wendy McClosky (SERVE at University of North Carolina, Greensboro),
who provided the examples in Appendix B; and to Dr. Stanley Nyirenda
(Western Michigan University), Dr. Andrew McConney (Western Oregon
State College), Dr. Joyce Annunziata (Dade County Public Schools, Florida),
and Dr. Audrey Kleinsasser (University of Wyoming) for their detailed and
helpful reviews in the formative stages of this manuscript's preparation.
And for her editorial assistance, thanks to Ms. Sally Veeder.

PETER W. AIRASIAN
Boston College, Massachusetts

ARLEN R. GULLICKSON
Western Michigan University, Kalamazoo

About the Authors

Peter W. Airasian received his A.B. from Harvard College in chemistry and his A.M. and Ph.D. from the University of Chicago in educational measurement and evaluation. He is currently Professor and Chair of the Counseling, Developmental Psychology, and Research Methods Department at Boston College, where he has been a faculty member for 27 years. His primary teaching responsibilities are undergraduate preservice classroom assessment courses and graduate courses in assessment and teacher evaluation. He is author or coauthor of *Minimal Competency Testing* (1979), *School Effectiveness: A Reassessment of the Evidence* (1980), *The Effects of Standardized Testing* (1982), *Classroom Assessment* (2nd ed., 1994), and *Assessment in the Classroom* (1996). He has taught chemistry and biology at English High School in Boston. He is currently working on teacher self-evaluation issues and strategies and applications of performance-based assessments.

Arlen R. Gullickson received his B.A. and M.A. from the University of Northern Iowa and his Ph.D. from the University of Colorado. He is Professor of Education and Chief of Staff of the Evaluation Center at Western Michigan University. From 1991 through January 1996, he served as Associate Director for the national Center for Research on Educational Accountability and Teacher Evaluation (CREATE). He serves as President of the new Consortium for Research on Educational Accountability and Teacher Evaluation, an international group dedicated to the improvement of personnel and program evaluation in schools, and is Vice Chairman of the Joint Committee on Standards for Educational Evaluation. He currently serves the Department of Education as a member of its Program Effectiveness Panel. He has authored or coauthored approximately 40 journal articles and book chapters.

Introduction

The *Teacher Self-Evaluation Tool Kit* provides an introduction to the rationale for and the application of teacher self-evaluation. Teacher self-evaluation encourages teachers to examine their own personal teaching activities and recognizes that teachers' main reason for engaging in evaluation is to understand and improve their own practice. Simply put, teacher self-evaluation is the process of a teacher, alone or with colleagues, undertaking self-examination of his or her own teaching in areas identified by the teacher, using methods selected by the teacher, and employing standards defined by the teacher.

In this book, we provide a context for self-evaluation by briefly addressing three questions: What is teacher self-evaluation? Why is teacher self-evaluation important? and, What do we know about teacher self-evaluation? We then describe common strategies used in teacher self-evaluation and provide 19 examples of simple, formal self-evaluation procedures that can help teachers learn about their teaching beliefs, knowledge, practices, and effectiveness. The main body of the book concludes with suggestions for getting started with self-evaluation.

We have purposely used "tool kit" in the title of the book. A tool kit contains tools useful for accomplishing tasks. We have provided some examples of self-evaluation tools in our tool kit. But a tool kit can grow as more tools are added to it, not only in terms of the number of tools but also in the number of tasks the tool kit permits one to accomplish. We view this tool kit as something that should be expanded, refined, and adapted by teachers as they find their own "tools" to help them understand and improve their practice. We hope this self-evaluation tool kit will provoke interest, use, expansion, and personalization by teachers who use it.

1 What Is Teacher Self-Evaluation?

Teacher self-evaluation is a process in which teachers make judgments about the adequacy and effectiveness of their own knowledge, performance, beliefs, or effects for the purpose of self-improvement. Teacher self-evaluation focuses on personal practice and recognizes that teachers' main reasons for engaging in professional development derive from their own teaching assignments, their own experiences of what it means to be a teacher, and their own need to make sense of and improve the daily experiences of teaching. Given this focus, it is obvious that the teacher is at the center of the self-evaluation process. In self-evaluation, the teacher becomes responsible for examining and improving his or her own practice. It is the teacher who collects, interprets, and judges information bearing on personal practice. It is the teacher who frames criteria and standards to judge the adequacy of his or her beliefs, knowledge, skills, and effectiveness. It is the teacher who decides on the nature of professional development activities to be undertaken. Teacher self-evaluation is evaluation of the teacher by the teacher and for the teacher.

Most evaluations carried out in classrooms are not teacher self-evaluations because they are not specifically focused on the teacher. In the classroom, teachers evaluate a wide array of things and make many kinds of decisions. Often, these classroom evaluations focus on pupils, classroom climate, and instructional resources and strategies, not on the teacher's own actions or beliefs. Teacher self-evaluation occurs when the focus of evaluation is directed away from pupils and instructional materials to the teacher himself or herself.

When a teacher asks, "Are they paying attention to my lesson?" the teacher is not self-evaluating. When the teacher asks, "Are they not paying attention to my lesson because I misjudged their readiness for the topic?"

2

the teacher is self-evaluating. The focus in the first question is on the pupils, whereas in the second the focus is on the teacher. One teacher summed up this distinction when she said,

> Then I realized that I am working in the dark. . . . I have been teaching for almost a full year now and I don't know much about my teaching. I gave a number of tests to pupils to find out how they were doing, but I did not use the results as a source of feedback for myself. (Kremer-Hayon, 1993, p. 47)

A defining aspect of any kind of evaluation is that it produces a decision or judgment about the person or object being evaluated. Thus teacher self-evaluation involves teachers making decisions about themselves and their practice. It is also important to note that processes like asking questions about one's practice, reflecting on one's practice, and interpreting one's practice are not, individually or in combination, teacher self-evaluation. Although each of these processes is used in teacher self-evaluation, self-evaluation only occurs when questions, reflections, and interpretations lead a teacher to make a decision about practice. Thus the function of self-evaluation is to help teachers identify and make decisions about the strengths and weaknesses of their practice, with the intent of improving it.

Teacher self-evaluation is a formative, not a summative, activity (McColskey & Egelson, 1993). Summative evaluations are usually performed by outsiders to the classroom for the purpose of making a judgment about the overall quality of a teacher's classroom performance. Summative evaluations become part of a teacher's personnel file and are used mainly for organizational decision making. Alternatively, formative evaluations are intended to provide information to help teachers improve on an ongoing basis. This usually means evaluation of more narrow aspects of teaching than are typically evaluated in summative evaluations. The context for collecting formative information about one's teaching is personal and nonjudgmental. In formatively oriented self-evaluation, the teacher controls both the aspects of practice to be examined and the method of examination.

The actual process of self-evaluation can be described in terms of four steps or stages, which may occur formally or informally as a teacher proceeds with self-evaluation.

1. *Problem identification or delineation.* In this stage, a problem or question about practice arises from a sense of discomfort, curiosity, or a desire to change. The teacher then should focus on the issue to be addressed, identify appropriate information to collect, and determine criteria that can help identify success or progress toward reaching the desired end. The key question is: What will be evaluated?

2. *Information gathering or obtaining.* In this stage, the data or information needed to inform the area of practice under study is collected and organized. The data collected may be formal or informal, but collection of some formal evidence is strongly recommended. This stage serves to provide teachers with an awareness of their practice that can then serve as a basis for teacher reflection and interpretation. The key question is: What information will be gathered?

3. *Reflection and decision making.* After reflecting on and interpreting the information gathered, the teacher makes a decision regarding the practice, belief, or effect under examination. The key question is: What is the meaning of the information for my teaching?

4. *Application and change.* In this stage, plans are made to carry out needed changes in practice deriving from the prior stages. The key question is: What action, if any, is now needed?

Thus self-evaluation should (a) have a clear focus, (b) collect information that will provide teachers with an objective awareness of their practice, (c) provide opportunity for teacher reflection, (d) result in a decision about practice, and (e) lead to strategies to improve teaching, if necessary. Self-evaluation is related, but not necessarily identical to, concepts such as the reflective practitioner, reflection on practice, teacher connoisseurship and criticism, teacher research, self-understanding, educational action research, and analysis of practice. All of these approaches seek to put teachers in the center of assessing their own practice.

Underlying teacher self-evaluation are the following beliefs (Airasian & Gullickson, 1994; Osterman & Kottkamp, 1993):

1. Teachers need professional growth opportunities.
2. Teachers want to improve their practice and knowledge; teachers want and need information about their knowledge, performance, and effectiveness.
3. Teachers are capable of assuming responsibility for much of their own professional growth and development, given time, encouragement, and resources.
4. Collaboration enriches professional growth and development.

It is important to note that despite the importance and usefulness of teacher self-evaluation, it is only part of a viable, ongoing program of teacher evaluation. Self-evaluation is evaluation for the teacher so that he or she may become aware of, reflect on, analyze, and make decisions about his or her practice. However, in most school settings, there is a need for other types of teacher evaluation because teachers are accountable to many constituents: (a) pupils and the community that are affected by their actions; (b) employers with whom they have contractual obligations; (c) their profession, which has its own standards and expectations; and (d) themselves as professionals. Although self-evaluation can fulfill some of these accountability needs, it cannot fulfill them all, necessitating that other forms of teacher evaluation be used to supplement teacher self-evaluation.

2 Why Is Teacher Self-Evaluation Important?

The nature of teacher evaluation is changing in response to four trends. First, the poor performance of American students on national and international tests has been associated, in part, with unsatisfactory performance by teachers. Second, the shift from an inspectorial to a collegial and reflective view of teacher development and evaluation has put teachers in the center of the teacher evaluation process. Third, new state certification and recertification mandates require continual teacher evaluation and increased teacher responsibility for demonstrating personal proficiency. Fourth, constructivist models of teaching and learning, which emphasize higher-order thinking and personal constructions of meaning, are introducing new and difficult-to-assess criteria for successful teaching, criteria that rely heavily on teacher evaluation and decision making about their practice. These four factors have focused attention on teacher evaluation and have substantially broadened its domain and techniques (Little, 1993).

In particular, teacher evaluation is shifting from an emphasis on certification and annual summative evaluations to a more balanced emphasis on summative and formative evaluations. This shift can be seen in efforts to extend assistance to new teachers, broaden career opportunities for experienced teachers, make teachers more responsible for demonstrating their own competence, introduce portfolio evaluation to foster teacher reflection, and provide opportunity for collegial and cooperative teacher activities such as site-based management and action research. All these efforts are designed to help teachers play an informed and active role in assessing and advancing their own practice.

Teacher self-evaluation is the most common of all forms of teacher evaluation (Airasian, Gullickson, Hahn, & Farland, 1995). The fact that it usually goes unnoticed because it is often carried out informally and unobtrusively should not blind us to its importance in the professional life of a teacher. It focuses on self-understanding and self-improvement, both critically important professional activities, especially in light of new teaching and learning models that call for teacher behaviors and decisions that cannot be reduced to the trainable skill sequences often found in inservice education. By recognizing teachers' self-evaluation activities, we acknowledge the contribution that teachers' own intellectual curiosity and concern make to the improvement of their teaching knowledge, beliefs, and activities.

Stufflebeam and Shinkfield (1985) suggest that the most important evaluations of professionals are those conducted by the professionals themselves. When teachers are encouraged to reflect on and revisit beliefs and practices, understanding and growth occur. Given opportunities to explore their beliefs, knowledge, practices, and effects makes teachers more likely to question their taken-for-granted expectations, norms, beliefs, and practices, especially if this exploration is conducted in a trusting, supportive environment. Clandinin and Connelly (1988) emphasize that self-knowledge and self-understanding are the keys to professional growth and that the best way to improve these is to give teachers more control and responsibility for self-evaluation. Gitlin et al. (1992) argue that building on such notions as the self-monitoring teacher and the teacher as classroom researcher represent the best ways to give teachers a true *voice* in their practice. Kuhn (1991) emphasizes the importance of thinking about one's theories and beliefs, not just applying them. Competent reasoning about one's beliefs and practice requires

> the ability to reflect on one's own thinking as an object of thought. In the absence of this ability, one's beliefs are utilized as a basis for organizing and interpreting experience, but only by means of this second-order, reflective thinking ability can one think about, evaluate, and hence be in a position to justify one's beliefs. Only in the latter case does one exercise control over one's beliefs. (Kuhn, 1991, pp. 13-14)

Although none of these commentators uses the term *self-evaluation* to describe the processes they recommend, all of the processes have self-evaluation at their heart.

Teacher self-evaluation is an important process for teachers to use because it

1. Is a professional responsibility
2. Focuses professional development and improvement on the classroom or school level where teachers have their greatest expertise and effect
3. Recognizes that organizational change is usually the result of individuals changing themselves and their personal practices, not of "top-down" mandates

4. Gives teachers voice, that is, a stake in and control over their own practice

5. Makes teachers aware of the strengths and weaknesses of their practice; it grows from the immediacy and complexity of the classroom, as do teachers' motives and incentives

6. Encourages ongoing teacher development and discourages unchanging classroom beliefs, routines, and methods

7. Treats the teacher as a professional and can improve teacher morale and motivation

8. Encourages collegial interactions and discussions about teaching (Airasian & Gullickson, 1994; McColskey & Egelson, 1993)

3   What Do We Know About Teacher Self-Evaluation?

Given its potential benefits, it is appropriate to ask what we know about teacher self-evaluation (Airasian et al., 1995; Kremer-Hayon, 1993). This chapter summarizes current knowledge.

What Are the Ways Teachers Self-Evaluate?

We know that not all teacher decisions are self-evaluations; self-evaluation requires that a teacher makes decisions about his or her own practice. We know that questions, reflections, and interpretations about practice contribute to self-evaluation but are not self-evaluation per se. We know that there are many avenues through which teachers self-evaluate. We know that some of these avenues provide more valid and accurate self-evaluations than others (Airasian et al., 1995).

We know that the majority of teachers' self-evaluations result from the spontaneously occurring ebb and flow of classroom activities—what Schon (1983) has termed "reflection in action." These evaluations (a) occur during an ongoing classroom activity, (b) arise spontaneously from the activity, (c) can produce a decision during the activity, and (d) are usually intuitive and tacit. Teachers' tacit, in-action reflections are important in shaping their practice and teaching beliefs, but they also have many characteristics that hamper their usefulness as a self-evaluation strategy. The unexpressed, fleeting nature of reflection in action makes it difficult to study and model; the amount of time available to reflect on any particular action event is very small, leading to brief and often shallow reflections and decisions; and the transient nature of reflection in action episodes can result in superficial, expedient decisions that lead to simplistic explanations and heuristics. Furthermore, what is reflected on and evaluated is controlled not by the teacher but by the spontaneous flow of events transpiring in the classroom. Thus reflection in action is reactive, not proactive. This reactivity serves to narrow one's view of practice because unless an aspect of practice arises spontaneously, problems of practice may be overlooked or not identified as being problems by a teacher.

We also know that not all teacher reflection and self-evaluation is based on spontaneously occurring classroom events. Some reflection and self-evaluation takes place post hoc, out of the immediacy of practice. This form of teacher reflection and self-evaluation is divorced in time from the factors that prompted the need for reflection and evaluation. Thus post hoc reflection on action (a) occurs out of practice, (b) involves conscious deliberation knowingly engaged in, and (c) can produce a decision about practice. However, in spite of its more contemplative, reflective nature, there are limitations to its use as a self-evaluation approach.

Self-evaluation resulting from post hoc reflection is highly dependent on teachers' recall of things reflected on. It seems likely, however, that teachers are no different from other people who reflect on their activities and actions, insofar as a substantial number of both the reflections and decisions made from the reflections are forgotten from one day to the next. Furthermore, reflection subsequent to action is hampered by many of the same contextual factors that limit the effectiveness of reflection in action. Both are action driven. Moreover, even with conscious deliberation, reflection still takes place in a closed system in which the teacher is both the evaluator and the evaluatee, with no counterbalancing external or non-teacher-generated information at hand. Regardless of whether the reflection is done during or after classroom action, there is nothing to validate or contradict the reflections and subsequent self-evaluations the teacher makes. This lack of external information is important because teachers' criteria, standards, and interpretations of events and outcomes are influenced by their preexisting beliefs and experiences, which they use to provide the interpretive framework needed to label and categorize new reflective situations. Frequently, such preconceptions preempt adequate teacher reflection on a situation of concern.

We know that the least used form of self-evaluation occurs when teachers enhance reflection based solely on personal perceptions and interpretations with more formal external evidence about practice. This evidence may be gathered in many forms and in many ways: from colleagues, students, records, and so on. The use of such external, formal information about practice is strongly recommended in this book for a variety of reasons, the most important being that it allows the teacher to obtain information that he or she can use to independently validate or corroborate his or her own perceptions and interpretations regarding practice. The remainder of this book is devoted to discussing the factors and strategies that can help teachers produce this enhanced reflection, awareness of practice, and self-evaluation.

What Are Commonly Used Self-Evaluation Procedures?

We know that there are a variety of formal teacher evaluation tools that can be used to enhance teacher reflection and self-evaluation. Self-reflective questionnaires and checklists, audio- or videotaping with analysis (e.g., micro-teaching), student-feedback questionnaires, portfolio preparations, student performance data, peer review, and other structured approaches are all useful sources of formal information for teachers' self-evaluation (Airasian & Gullickson, 1994; Angelo & Cross, 1993; McColskey & Egelson, 1993). However, many of these tools are not widely used because the demands of teaching, the constancy of classroom involvement, and the need for immediate decision making often inhibit teachers' desires to undertake self-evaluation. There are many viable techniques and strategies that teachers can use in meaningful and manageable ways to inform and improve their practice. We will present a sample of these techniques and strategies later in this chapter.

What Is the Role of Principal Evaluations in Teacher Self-Evaluation?

We know that the formal, annual principal or department head teacher evaluations are regarded by most teachers as not useful for fostering self-reflection, analysis of practice, and professional development. The brevity of the typical observation, the observer's lack of knowledge of the classroom culture, the lack of specific suggestions for improvement, and the lack of support for improvement efforts are all cited by teachers to explain why these evaluations provide little impetus for self-evaluation. Many principals recognize and describe the same limitations in these evaluations as do teachers.

What Factors Influence Teachers Efforts to Carry Out Self-Evaluation?

We know that the motivation and willingness needed to engage in and sustain teacher self-evaluation are influenced by both personal and situational factors. Teachers' awareness of their teaching performance, sense of self-efficacy, values and beliefs about education, risk-taking tolerance, and ability to be objective about themselves influence engagement and persistence in self-evaluation activities. But the success of self-evaluation does not rest solely on teacher characteristics. Efforts to carry out self-evaluation are also influenced by situational factors such as principal's and colleagues' support for self-evaluation, resources and time to examine and improve practice, collegial trust and openness, and the clarity and detail of descriptions provided about teaching practice. If self-evaluation is to flourish and move beyond the informal, somewhat narrow perspective that now dominates its conduct, it will be necessary to situate it in a nurturing environment.

What Is the Nature of Self-Evaluation Standards and Criteria?

We know that the standards and criteria teachers use to guide their self-evaluation decisions tend to be tacit, intuitive, idiosyncratic, and changeable. Teachers are more likely to report making a decision because it felt right or intuitively seemed correct than on the basis of more formal and objective criteria or standards. There is an absence of well-defined standards and criteria for teacher self-evaluation, just as there is for teacher evaluation in general. As noted, the complexity and constancy of classroom events encourage teachers to prefer quick and simple self-evaluation criteria such as posture and facial expressions. Unfortunately, these secondary criteria often lead teachers' self-evaluations astray. The issue here is not that teachers lack self-evaluation standards and criteria. They do not. But the fact that these standards and criteria tend to be tacit and idiosyncratic prevents teachers from articulating them and being accountable for their decisions, even to themselves.

What Are Some Barriers to Teacher Self-Evaluation?

We know that there are numerous barriers that inhibit teachers from carrying out self-evaluations (Gullickson, Airasian, & Assaff, 1994). Some of these were described in the first part of this chapter. In addition, pre- and inservice teacher preparation rarely includes information and practice in self-evaluation. Lack of time to engage in meaningful self-evaluation is a major barrier, generally forcing teachers to rely on superficial, easily observed—but often invalid—indicators of practice. Moreover, self-evaluation is about *self*, and teachers' vested interest in the results of their practice can lead to biased, incomplete, or inadequate descriptions. Without external evidence about practice, teachers' preconceptions and beliefs often preempt careful observation of practice or focus teachers on aspects of practice that reinforce their preconceptions and beliefs.

A second set of barriers to valid teacher self-evaluation pertains to the inferences teachers derive from information about their practice (Kuhn, 1991; Nisbett & Ross, 1980). Teachers, like most people, often generalize from inadequate information; overestimate the accuracy of their observations and interpretations of practice; rely on simplistic, one-variable explanations for complex phenomena; and tend to generate interpretations that support their prior views, thereby transferring responsibility for problems of practice from the teacher to some other source. All of these barriers can prevent teachers from recognizing that they are performing unsatisfactorily, thus inhibiting the conduct of meaningful teacher self-evaluation. Figure 3.1 summarizes what we know about teacher self-evaluation.

1. Teachers indicate that they do self-evaluate and value the process.

2. The vast majority of teacher-described self-evaluation is focused on spontaneous and intuitive judgments about the flow of classroom activities.

3. Some teachers do collect and use formal information to enhance their personal perceptions and guide reflection, understanding, and improvement of practice.

4. Teachers use a variety of formal self-evaluation strategies (e.g., micro-teaching, peer review, self-reflective questionnaires), but many of these strategies are not used because teachers report lack of time to implement, analyze, and interpret the information provided.

5. For most teachers, annual principal or department head evaluations of teaching are regarded as not useful for self-evaluation because of their brevity, lack of specific suggestions for improvement, and lack of resources needed to improve.

6. Motivation and willingness to participate and persevere in self-evaluation activities depends on personal (e.g., awareness of teaching practice, sense of self-efficacy, and risk-taking tolerance) and situational (e.g., collegial and administrative support, trust, and openness) factors.

7. The standards and criteria teachers use to guide self-evaluation tend to be tacit, idiosyncratic, and changeable. Teachers rely more on intuition and feel when judging themselves than on more formal information and standards.

8. There are many personal and situational factors that present barriers to the conduct of valid, meaningful teacher self-evaluation.

Figure 3.1. What Is Known About Teacher Self-Evaluation

4 Strategies and Examples for Teacher Self-Evaluation

The preceding chapters have provided information about what teacher self-evaluation is, why it is important, and what we know about its practice. In this chapter, we present specific examples of strategies that can be used to carry out meaningful and useful self-evaluation. The examples are meant to be illustrative of possibilities, not exhaustive and all-encompassing. The number of specific self-evaluation strategies that could be generated is unlimited. We expect and hope that our examples will be altered, adapted, or extended according to individual teachers' needs. Suggestions for how to do this are offered in Chapter 5.

Two fundamental criteria guided the selection of the examples to be presented. First, the selected examples are formal, in the sense that they produce some tangible record or information for self-evaluation. The nature and source of the information can vary considerably, but in all cases, the aim is to produce tangible information to use for analyzing and making decisions about practice. Although personal observation and interpretation are useful, they are much more effective when used in conjunction with other, more formally obtained evidence. It is important to note, however, that the focus on formal approaches does not mean that the approaches have to be complicated, time consuming, or controlled by others.

Second, the examples are aimed at helping teachers to obtain an awareness of their practice, including their beliefs, knowledge, activities, and effects. Much of the current discussion about teacher development emphasizes teacher reflection and introspection as the path to change and improvement. Although reflection and introspection are important aspects of professional development, they are insufficient to guarantee improvement. The missing link between reflection or introspection and the self-evaluation decisions that lead to professional development is an objective awareness of one's practice. Before we can meaningfully reflect on practice, before we can chart avenues of needed change, before we can make meaningful decisions about practice, it is necessary that we have a clear awareness of our teaching practice: our actions, assumptions, beliefs, and effects. Awareness is essential for change, and although reflection may help awareness, it does so much more productively when it is based on formal information about practice. Thus the self-evaluation examples presented here will produce formal evidence that teachers can use to obtain an explicit awareness of their practice. The specific examples are derived from the following eight general self-evaluation strategies. Resource A presents a more detailed examination of these strategies.

1. *Teacher self-reflection tools* are designed to be completed by the teacher to allow him or her to evaluate performance in the areas identified on the self-reflection tool. These tools usually are in the form of a checklist, rating scale, or questionnaire.

2. *Media recording and analysis* use medialike audio- or videotape to record a sample of teacher performance for subsequent analysis by the teacher, peers, or both. Microteaching is one example of media recording.

3. *Student feedback tools* are similar to the self-reflection tools except that pupils instead of the teacher complete the forms. Teacher-made questionnaires, Minute Surveys, and journals are examples of sources of student feedback.

4. *Teacher portfolios* are prepared by teachers to provide evidence about their beliefs, knowledge, skills, and effectiveness. The process of collecting and analyzing portfolio pieces provides another form of self-evaluation evidence.

5. *Student performance data* include all student products that can be used to help the teacher assess his or her own instructional effectiveness. Test results (teacher-made or standardized), essays, classroom projects, and the like are examples of student performance data.

6. *External or peer observation* involves having a peer or colleague observe, assess, and provide suggestions about an aspect of the teacher's practice such as questioning behavior, lesson organization, or feedback to students.

7. *Journaling* requires the teacher to maintain and reflect on a record of classroom events or activities with the intent of recognizing recurring problems, themes, successes, and needs.

8. *Collegial dialogue, experience sharing, and joint problem solving* all encourage collaboration among teachers to discuss common problems, share

procedures and strategies, and compare perceptions. Exposure to the ideas and practices of colleagues is a potent strategy for teacher reflection and change.

The self-evaluation examples vary in many ways. However, there are some underlying themes that should be kept in mind when applying any self-evaluation tool. First, self-evaluation approaches that obtain feedback from students should protect the anonymity of the student respondents. Students should not be required to sign their names or provide other clues to their identity. Maintaining student anonymity protects and encourages them to provide the honest feedback needed for viable self-evaluation.

Second, in selecting areas to self-evaluate, focus on narrow aspects of teaching rather than more general ones. Note that all the following examples seek to provide information about well-defined and limited aspects of teaching. Thus it is more productive and diagnostic to inquire about one's questioning strategies or beliefs about learning than it is to inquire about one's general teaching competence or instructional approaches.

Third, whenever possible, build a comparison into self-evaluations. Before administering a student feedback tool, videotaping a lesson, or asking a colleague to observe you, make predictions of what the main outcomes will be. If possible, write these down. Then, when you get the actual results, you can compare them to your predictions. Making predictions will help you be more objective in interpreting self-evaluation results and will highlight significant areas of need or excellence.

Fourth, recognize that no single strategy can provide all the information needed to self-evaluate teaching. Different self-evaluation strategies are useful for evaluating different areas, as shown in the examples that follow.

Each of the examples is categorized in terms of (a) the area of teaching it assesses—beliefs, knowledge, practice, or effects—and (b) the general self-evaluation strategy it exemplifies (see Table 4.1). Some examples can be categorized in more than one way.

TABLE 4.1 Categorization of Self-Evaluation Examples

Self-Evaluation Strategy	Area Assessed			
	Beliefs	Knowledge	Practice	Effects
1. Teacher self-reflection tool	Examples 1, 12	Examples 7, 12	Examples 5, 7, 8, 16, 19	
2. Media recording and analysis			Examples 4, 6, 9	
3. Student feedback tool	Example 1		Examples 2, 3, 4, 9, 10, 13, 17	Examples 3, 13, 17
4. Teacher portfolios		Example 15	Example 15	Example 15
5. Student performance data			Example 9	Examples 11, 18
6. External observation			Examples 4, 6, 8, 9, 14	
7. Journaling				
8. Collegial dialogue and problem solving			Example 14	Example 18

NOTE: Some examples may fit in more than one strategy.

Example 1

Area Assessed: Beliefs

SELF-EVALUATION STRATEGY:
TEACHER SELF-REFLECTION OR STUDENT FEEDBACK TOOL

The following statements are about classroom learning. Read each statement and circle the option that best describes your belief (SA = *strongly agree*; A = *agree*; U = *uncertain*; D = *disagree*; SD = *strongly disagree*). There are no right or wrong answers.

1. Most classes exhibit a wide variety of abilities and learning styles.
   SA A U D SD

2. To learn best, pupils should be active participants in the learning process.
   SA A U D SD

3. Pupils achieve better when they know the goal, see models that exemplify good practice, and know the standards by which they will be judged.
   SA A U D SD

4. The teacher should determine classroom rules, goals, instructional topics, teaching methods, and evaluations.
   SA A U D SD

5. The main purpose of teaching is to help students accumulate information about a subject area.
   SA A U D SD

6. Most pupils learn and can be taught in very similar ways.
   SA A U D SD

Review your answers, and list ways you practice your beliefs about learning in your own instruction.

List some areas in which your actions during instruction do not mirror your beliefs about learning as well as you would like. How might you narrow the gap between your beliefs and your actions during instruction?

Obtain a score for your teaching beliefs. For statements 1, 2, and 3, give yourself 5 points for an SA response, 4 points for an A response, 3 points for a U response, 2 points for a D response, and 1 point for an SD response. For statements 4, 5, and 6, reverse this scoring by giving 5 points for an SD response, 4 for a D response, 3 for a U response, 2 for an A response, and 1 for an SA response. Total your score.

If you had a high score on the belief scale, your classroom should manifest many of the following characteristics, not just occasionally but as integral parts of instruction.

- Encouraging discussion of new ideas
- Encouraging divergent, not one-answer thinking
- Providing choices in assigned tasks
- Giving students opportunities to reexamine and revise their work and knowledge
- Discussing goals, criteria, and standards with students before evaluation
- Letting students help determine criteria and standards
- Providing examples or models of good and bad performance to students
- Allowing peer evaluation and self-evaluation
- Fostering group opportunities and cooperation
- Providing more diagnostic information to students

If you obtained a low score, your classroom should manifest a teacher-centered instructional climate, with unitary instruction, assignments, and evaluations.

How well are your beliefs mirrored in practice? Reflect on the gap between your stated beliefs about learning and your actual classroom practices. What might you do to more closely align your beliefs with your practice?

To add another dimension to consideration of your teaching beliefs in relation to your teaching actions, you could reword the six belief statements so that your students could respond to them. Make your own projections of how students will respond before asking them to respond to the reworded statements. This will give you an opportunity to compare your own classroom perceptions to those of your students.

When soliciting student feedback, it is extremely important that the students be granted anonymity by not having to sign their names, having a student collect the feedback, and even, if possible, having students summarize the results.

Example 2

Area Assessed: Practice

SELF-EVALUATION STRATEGY: STUDENT FEEDBACK TOOL

Here are five statements that describe life in this classroom. For each item, circle the letter in front of the phrase that best states how you feel about being in the classroom.

1. When I am in class, I usually am
   a. Wide awake and interested
   b. Pretty interested, kind of bored part of the time
   c. Not very interested, bored a lot of the time
   d. Bored, don't like being here

2. How often does the teacher act friendly toward the class?
   a. Always
   b. Some of the time
   c. Sometimes
   d. Hardly ever

3. How much does the teacher care about whether you learn in this class?
   a. A lot
   b. Some
   c. Not very much

4. How often does the teacher make clear what is expected of you in assignments?
   a. Always
   b. Most of the time
   c. Sometimes
   d. Hardly ever

5. When you get something wrong on a test or assignment, how often does your teacher explain what you did wrong?
   a. Always
   b. Most of the time
   c. Sometimes
   d. Hardly ever

In using this or other student surveys of classroom practices and attitudes, teachers should follow these guidelines:

- When soliciting student feedback, it is extremely important that the students be granted anonymity by not having to sign their names, having a student collect the feedback, and even, if possible, having students summarize the results.

- Make a personal projection of how students in general will respond *before* you look at actual student responses.

- Compare your projection to the students' responses and use the information to reinforce existing practice or to identify ways to improve existing practice and attitudes.

Example 3

Area Assessed: Practice or Effects

SELF-EVALUATION STRATEGY: STUDENT FEEDBACK TOOL

The Minute Survey is a flexible and simple strategy for getting feedback from pupils regarding various aspects of classroom activities (Angelo & Cross, 1993). To conduct a Minute Survey, the teacher sets aside 2 or 3 minutes at the end of the class to survey the students about some aspect of the lesson. The teacher asks each student to take out a piece of paper (or, in early grades, raise their hand or make some indication) and poses one or two questions to the class about the lesson. Students respond anonymously. For example, the teacher might ask the students to do one or two of the following activities:

1. Write two things they learned from the lesson.
2. Write one question they would like to have answered about the lesson.
3. Indicate whether they would like you to spend more time on this lesson.
4. State how confident they are about doing tonight's homework on this lesson.
5. Rate the success of the example presented to reinforce the lesson's main point.
6. Rate how well the reading assignment prepared them for today's lesson.
7. Solve one or two problems or calculations similar to those taught in the lesson.

There are, of course, many other questions a teacher could ask pupils about a lesson, an assignment, a homework exercise, a field trip, a video presentation, a demonstration, or even a test. However, to make the use of the Minute Survey most informative, the following guidelines should be followed.

- Let the students reply anonymously.
- Keep the amount of writing requested of the students small. Don't ask students to write responses to four or five questions. The Minute Sur-

vey is meant to be completed in a short time and hence should focus on one or two aspects of the lesson.

- Before reading over the responses to the Minute Survey, try to answer the question yourself, based on your perception of the lesson. For example, what do you (the teacher) think will be the two most important things most students will say they learned, or the one question most students will want answered, or how well the example you showed helped students to learn? Answering the question yourself will provide a check on your observational impressions in light of students actual responses.

- Read the responses; compare them to your own prediction and, depending on the responses, use the information to reteach, answer questions, reexplain, or move on to the next topic.

Example 4

Area Assessed: Practice

SELF-EVALUATION STRATEGY: MEDIA RECORDING,
EXTERNAL OBSERVATION, OR STUDENT FEEDBACK TOOL

There are many ways to obtain information about the nature and content of classroom discourse. One can have a colleague observe a lesson or two and provide information about who talks most and about what, the quality of questions asked, the reinforcement and encouragement given students, and so on. One can also poll pupils to obtain their impressions of the nature and content of classroom discourse. One can use media such as audio- or videotape to obtain and subsequently analyze discourse. One advantage of media is that a permanent record of performance is obtained, one that can be examined and reexamined. Often, when we are engaged and engrossed in the process of teaching, we are not aware of how much we talk, to whom, why, and with what purpose.

Regardless of the method used to obtain information on classroom discourse, it is useful to do two things to increase the usefulness of the information:

- State a set of questions you want to answer before collecting information.
- Answer the questions yourself before you examine the information collected.

Sample questions that might guide analysis of discourse during a lesson include the following:

1. What proportion of time is spent in teacher talk?
2. Are there differences in the amount of talk from high- and low-ability students, males and females, and so on?
3. What is the proportion of social or personal chat compared to on-task talk?
4. How many different students participate in discourse?
5. How much time is spent setting up and explaining the purpose of the lesson?
6. How much time is spent summing up and responding to student questions?

Example 5

Area Assessed: Practice

SELF-EVALUATION STRATEGY: TEACHER SELF-REFLECTION TOOL

This questionnaire is intended to help you identify and reflect on your current and future professional development activities. Answer each question by circling the term that most describes your level of agreement, and then list current and planned activities in the spaces provided.

1. I am actively involved in developing my command of the knowledge base of teaching.

   strongly agree   agree   disagree   strongly disagree

   Topics I am currently working on   Topics I will work on next

   _____   _____

   _____   _____

2. I am actively engaged in reflecting on issues related to myself as a teacher and my professional role.

   strongly agree   agree   disagree   strongly disagree

   Topics I am currently reflecting on   Topics I plan to reflect on next

   _____   _____

   _____   _____

3. I am actively engaged in developing my repertoire of specific teaching and assessment practices.

   strongly agree   agree   disagree   strongly disagree

   Topics I am currently learning   Topics I plan to learn next

   _____   _____

   _____   _____

4. What is the one area of teaching in which you think you most need professional development? What evidence leads you to identify this particular need?

Example 6

Area Assessed: Practice

SELF-EVALUATION STRATEGY: MEDIA RECORDING
OR EXTERNAL OBSERVATION

This self-evaluation strategy focuses on important aspects of a cooperative learning lesson. It can be used by an individual teacher who could videotape and analyze his or her performance. It can be used by having a colleague or administrator sit in on the lesson and observe and record the teacher's performance in light of the selected important aspects listed below. If an observer is used, it would be helpful for that person to have some idea of the focus of the cooperative group lesson.

Observe the teacher's performance during the lesson in terms of the following criteria. Rate each criterion as *excellent, good,* or *needs improvement* by writing an X under the appropriate category. If possible, jot down suggestions or significant observations to point out to the teacher later.

COOPERATIVE LEARNING LESSON

Activity	Excellent	Good	*Needs* Improvement
Appropriateness of topic for students			
Materials ready at start of lesson			
Groups preformed or formed efficiently			
Goals and purpose of lesson explained			
Procedures for cooperation explained			
Desired group activities explained			
Smooth transition into group activities			
Teams helped during lesson			
All teams visited at least once			
Lesson ended with summary or directions for continuation			
Other comments on strong and weak points of the lesson:			

Example 7

Area Assessed: Practice or Knowledge

SELF-EVALUATION STRATEGY: TEACHER SELF-REFLECTION TOOL

Often, the simple task of rating oneself can lead to reflection about what one really knows or can do and what one needs more knowledge or skill to perform as well as one would like. In carrying out such self-ratings, it is better to rate specific areas of knowledge and skill than more general ones. The more specific the knowledge or skill, the easier it is to focus on its improvement, if necessary. Thus, rather than rating one's assessment and evaluation skills in general, the following instrument is useful in focusing on more detailed aspects of assessment and evaluation skills.

Rate your knowledge or skill as *high, medium,* or *low* for each of the following. For each skill, put an X under the appropriate rating category.

LEVEL OF KNOWLEDGE OR SKILL

Understanding or Skill	*High*	*Medium*	*Low*
My understanding of the effects of			
My grades on students			
Biases in my grading procedures			
Importance of grades to parents			
Norm-referenced versus criterion-referenced grades			
What my grades actually represent			
The fairness of my grading system			
My skill at			
Diagnosing students' prior knowledge			
Providing relevant feedback			
Preparing students for my tests			
Linking my teaching to my tests			
Including nonrote items in my tests			
Selecting valid textbook tests			
Scoring essay items fairly			

Select one area of knowledge and skill that you rated low, and write a plan for how you could go about improving this knowledge or skill.

Example 8

Area Assessed: Practice

SELF-EVALUATION STRATEGY: TEACHER SELF-REFLECTION TOOL
OR EXTERNAL OBSERVATION

The purpose of this strategy is to provide a simple and quick format to review a lesson that you have taught. All teachers have impressions about the success of a particular class or lesson they have just taught: This part went well, this part was too long, I lost them at this point, and so on. Usually, these self-critiques are lost when we move on to the next class or lesson. It might be helpful to compile information on the strong and weak points of lessons to view over time for patterns and for comparison to student feedback from Minute Surveys or other strategies.

This form could also be completed by a peer who observed the lesson.

LESSON REVIEW

1. What was the single best aspect of this lesson? Why?

2. What was the single most disappointing aspect of this lesson? Why?

3. What is one thing you can do next time to improve this lesson or lessons like it?

Over time, one might look over these lesson reviews to determine whether there are patterns of strengths and weaknesses; whether these patterns are consistent across classes, lessons, or subject areas; and whether improvements made in prior lessons were successful. There is also potential to increase teachers' repertoire of instructional strategies through the implementation of new practices to overcome past problems.

Example 9

Area Assessed: Practice

SELF-EVALUATION STRATEGY: STUDENT PERFORMANCE DATA, MEDIA
RECORDING, EXTERNAL OBSERVATION, OR STUDENT FEEDBACK TOOL

This strategy is aimed at identifying the nature and quality of the feedback teachers provide to students. Feedback may come in different forms for different assignments and subject areas, so this strategy may be usefully employed in more than one subject area or context (e.g., homework, tests, class discussion).

Information to assess teacher feedback may be gathered by reviewing the comments on a set of student papers (reports, tests, drafts, etc.) after they have been graded or reviewed, tape- or video-recording a lesson, asking students for feedback, or having another teacher observe a lesson. In any case, some questions that should guide information gathering and analysis of feedback include the following:

1. How soon do I provide feedback on student papers and ideas?
2. How specific is the feedback? Do I use vague or general words or phrases in my feedback, such as "good," "poor vocabulary," or "Work on this"? Or do I use specific wording in my feedback that informs the student, such as "good combination of adjectives to convey meaning," "The vocabulary you use is stilted and reads like you've just picked obscure words from a thesaurus," or "Try to be sure to use singular verbs with singular subjects and plural verbs with plural subjects"?
3. Do I focus feedback on specific behaviors students can work on?
4. Do I show students how to perform correctly or give them examples of good performance?
5. Do I try to balance negative feedback with positive feedback?
6. Do I try to teach students to judge their own performances? Do I give them practice in doing this?

Once a teacher has a sense of his or her general practices in providing feedback, he or she can begin to consider whether these practices are consistent across various student groups (e.g., males-females, high ability–low ability).

Example 10

Area Assessed: Practice

SELF-EVALUATION STRATEGY: STUDENT FEEDBACK TOOL

This student-completed questionnaire can be used to help a teacher assess the environment of the classroom as perceived by the students. If the teacher predicts how students will respond before administering the questionnaire, he or she can compare student perceptions to his or her own perceptions.

This strategy can be used to gather information on many aspects of student perceptions.

Distribute the questionnaire to students and ask them to respond (anonymously) to each question by circling 1 for *seldom*, 2 for *sometimes*, and 3 for *always*.

HOW WE WORK TOGETHER

Do I praise your good work?	1	2	3
Do I like you?	1	2	3
Do I call on you when you raise your hand?	1	2	3
Do I work with you as much as with other students?	1	2	3
Do I grade your work fairly?	1	2	3
Do I like your work?	1	2	3
Do I explain clearly what I want done?	1	2	3
Do I give you enough time to do your work?	1	2	3
Do I help you when you need help?	1	2	3

When soliciting student feedback, it is extremely important that the students be granted anonymity by not having to sign their names, having a student collect the feedback, and, if possible, having students summarize the results.

Make and record your own projections of what the results will be before asking for student feedback.

Example 11

Area Assessed: Effects

SELF-EVALUATION STRATEGY: STUDENT PERFORMANCE DATA

This strategy is intended to promote thinking about both instruction and student learning. It is based on examination of and reflection on students' learning gains. It is predicated on the availability of chapter or unit tests that can serve as pretests and posttests. Most textbooks provide both an end-of-chapter assessment and a review assessment. The latter can serve the function of a preunit test and the former the function of a postunit test.

1. Plan your instruction on the unit or chapter as you normally would.
2. Administer the preunit test to students before instruction begins.
3. Score the tests, not just in terms of total score but by objective as well.
4. Based on the students' scores, determine the following:
    a. How well your original lesson plan fits the information from the pretest
    b. How you might have to revise the plan based on the pretest information
    c. A prediction of how the class will do after instruction
5. Teach the chapter, making revisions in your plan as needed.
6. Administer the posttest and score it.
7. Compare the students' pretest and posttest performance, examining both total score and individual objectives.
8. On the basis of the comparison, ask yourself:
    a. How did the class do as a whole relative to your prediction?
    b. In what areas (objectives) did the class learn well and what areas need improvement?
    c. Why did the class not learn some areas as well as others; what might explain the discrepancy in learning across objectives?
    d. What can I do next time to improve learning of those objectives?
9. Examine the performance of the three pupils who showed the least change in learning from the pretest to the posttest. What was the nature of their mistakes, and what could you do next time or in the next unit to help them improve?

Once you have collected and examined the pretest and posttest information, you will raise many additional questions and issues.

Example 12

Area Assessed: Knowledge or Beliefs

SELF-EVALUATION STRATEGY: TEACHER SELF-REFLECTION TOOL

This self-evaluation strategy asks you to rate your knowledge of some educational processes or activities. For each process or activity, indicate how familiar you are with how it could be applied in a classroom by circling one of the following terms: *very familiar, somewhat familiar, heard the term,* or *unfamiliar.*

1. How familiar are you with the classroom implications and applications of
   a. Alternative assessment
      very familiar   somewhat familiar   heard the term   unfamiliar
   b. Inclusion
      very familiar   somewhat familiar   heard the term   unfamiliar
   c. Multiple intelligences
      very familiar   somewhat familiar   heard the term   unfamiliar
   d. Portfolios
      very familiar   somewhat familiar   heard the term   unfamiliar
   e. Inquiry teaching
      very familiar   somewhat familiar   heard the term   unfamiliar
   f. Action research
      very familiar   somewhat familiar   heard the term   unfamiliar
   g. Advanced organizer
      very familiar   somewhat familiar   heard the term   unfamiliar
   h. Constructivism
      very familiar   somewhat familiar   heard the term   unfamiliar
   i. Higher-order thinking skills (HOTS)
      very familiar   somewhat familiar   heard the term   unfamiliar
   j. Metacognition
      very familiar   somewhat familiar   heard the term   unfamiliar

2. Which two of these processes or activities do you most want to learn more about?

3. Where or to whom in your school or district would you go to get the information you want?

Example 13

Area Assessed: Practice or Effects

SELF-EVALUATION STRATEGY: STUDENT FEEDBACK TOOL

At the end of the school year, a teacher could ask students to write a report about the work they have done during the year or their experiences in the classroom. The teacher could focus the report on particular issues of interest to him or her. For example, students could be asked about the activities they enjoyed most and least, the activities from which they learned the most and least, the variety of instructional approaches they experienced, what one aspect of instruction they would most like to change, how fair grading was, and so on.

It would be best not to have students include a large number of areas in their reports. Stick to the two or three questions or issues you are most curious or concerned about. It also would be useful, although not essential, to have the students give reasons for their answers.

The teacher would read the reports, look for patterns, and decide what changes ought to be made for succeeding classes.

The issues addressed in the report could extend to teacher characteristics (what the teacher could have done to help students learn more; what changes they would like to have seen in the teacher's instructional approach, grading practices, homework assignments, etc.).

This is a flexible and simple way to get student feedback on some issues of interest to the teacher.

This approach can be modified to provide information about a particular unit, activity, field trip, and so on (see Minute Survey in Example 3). The modifications made should

- Focus the students on narrow questions (e.g., What did you like most about the field trip? or What two new things did you learn from the field trip?)
- Have the students respond anonymously
- Make predictions of student responses *before* reading them to compare to the students actual responses
- Identify your successful and unsuccessful practices

Example 14

Area Assessed: Practice

SELF-EVALUATION STRATEGY: COLLEGIAL DIALOGUE
OR EXTERNAL OBSERVATION

On a separate sheet of paper, list one teaching skill that you especially wish to improve. Why did you select that skill?

Now list the particular aspects of that teaching skill you think you need to improve most.

List the names of one or two faculty members in your school who you think are accomplished in this skill and from whom you could get advice and suggestions about the particular aspects of the skill you wish to improve. If you cannot identify such a colleague, ask other teachers or your principal for suggestions.

Talk to these faculty members about the teaching skill you wish to improve. Alternatively, one or both of these faculty members could observe you and provide suggestions for improving the selected skill.

Example 15

Area Assessed: Practice, Knowledge, or Effects

SELF-EVALUATION STRATEGY: TEACHER PORTFOLIO

In simplest terms, a portfolio is a collection of pieces. The pieces that make up portfolios can vary widely, but in most cases they are collected for one of two purposes:

1. To document breadth of practice or competence
2. To document change or improvement in a particular area or skill

Thus a portfolio assembled to demonstrate the breadth of a teacher's practice would likely include teacher reflections, lesson plans, video- or audiotapes of lessons, samples of student work, examples of tests or assessments, reviews of journals describing new teaching knowledge, professional development activities, photographs, and other pieces that could help provide a broad view of the teacher and his or her entire practice.

Conversely, a portfolio assembled to document change or improvement would be much narrower, containing information about a single performance or product collected over time. For example, a teacher might have a colleague observe and rate her or his performance during a cooperative learning lesson, using the cooperative learning lesson criteria shown in Example 6. Using the feedback from a colleague, the teacher might plan another cooperative learning lesson and have a colleague (the same or a different one) observe and rate it, using the same set of criteria. The cycle of lesson, feedback, change, lesson could proceed through three or four iterations. At the end, the teacher would have three or four ratings of his or her cooperative learning lessons over time and be able to chart improvement in performance.

Obviously, there are many possible topics for portfolio self-evaluation. Here are a few examples of how portfolios can be used in self-evaluation. In all cases, the aim is to use portfolios to obtain a greater awareness of practice with an aim toward personal and professional improvement.

Broad, varied portfolios. Using the self-evaluation strategy shown in Example 12, a teacher could identify areas with which he or she is unfamiliar. Each week or month the teacher could read one or two articles on one of the unfamiliar areas and list two or three ways the new knowledge could be incorporated into her or his teaching. Over the course of a few months, a useful and varied portfolio of new knowledge and practices could be built up. A logical extension of this portfolio would be self-evaluation of the new teaching practices when they are tried.

After selecting a subject area (math, science, language arts, algebra, etc.), a teacher could construct a portfolio of different methods to teach and assess the varied topics in that area. The idea would be to develop a portfolio that contained new and alternative ways to teach and assess the topics covered and to try them out.

Improvement portfolios. Because improvement involves determining change over time, many of the self-evaluation tools described in this chapter can become the basis for an improvement portfolio if they are applied over time. For example, all the teacher self-evaluation tools (see Examples 1, 5, 7, 8, 12, 16, and 19) are viable approaches on which to base an improvement self-evaluation portfolio. Remember, it is the awareness of practice resulting from the application of a self-evaluation tool that is the spur to changed practice and subsequent reapplication of the self-evaluation tool.

Example 16

Area Assessed: Practice

SELF-EVALUATION STRATEGY: TEACHER SELF-REFLECTION TOOL

For each statement, circle the number that indicates your agreement or disagreement (5 = *strongly agree*; 4 = *agree*; 3 = *uncertain*; 2 = *disagree*; 1 = *strongly disagree*).

	SA	A	U	D	SD
1. I often try different instructional techniques in my classroom.	5	4	3	2	1
2. I am able to manage student misbehavior in an appropriate way.	5	4	3	2	1
3. I provide feedback to students that helps them understand how they can improve their performance.	5	4	3	2	1
4. I use many instructional resources to supplement the textbook.	5	4	3	2	1
5. I give students a chance to apply and use information in a way that goes beyond memorizing facts.	5	4	3	2	1
6. I have a clear sense of the individual needs of each of my students.	5	4	3	2	1
7. I consciously set high standards for my students and convey to them what my expectations are.	5	4	3	2	1
8. I have read an article that discussed a new teaching technique in the past week.	5	4	3	2	1
9. I have tried a new instructional strategy or approach in my class within the past 2 weeks.	5	4	3	2	1
10. Most of my assessments of students are done using paper-and-pencil tests.	5	4	3	2	1

SOURCE: Adapted from Teacher Self-Evaluation Form, Deep River Elementary School, Lee County, North Carolina, 1992.

After rating yourself, give a modified version of the form to students. Compare the results.

Alternatively, review lesson plans, tests, teaching methods, and so on to determine whether your actual practice mirrors your ratings.

Example 17

Area Assessed: Practice or Effects

SELF-EVALUATION STRATEGY: STUDENT FEEDBACK TOOL

Here are some sentences about your teacher and your classroom. Read each sentence and circle the number that best describes your belief (3 = *the sentence is always true*; 2 = *the sentence is sometimes true*; 1 = *the sentence is never true*).

1. My teacher listens to me.	3	2	1
2. I understand my teacher's rules.	3	2	1
3. My teacher helps me with my work when I don't understand something.	3	2	1
4. I learn lots of things in this class.	3	2	1
5. My teacher tests me on things I have been taught in class.	3	2	1
6. My teacher wants me to learn a lot.	3	2	1
7. My teacher answers my questions.	3	2	1
8. My teacher teaches me in many different ways.	3	2	1

SOURCE: Adapted from Student Survey, Deep River Elementary School, Lee County, North Carolina, 1992.

Example 18

Area Assessed: Effects

SELF-EVALUATION STRATEGY: STUDENT PERFORMANCE DATA
OR COLLEGIAL DIALOGUE

An often overlooked source of information about teaching success that can be a stimulus to improve teaching knowledge and skills is analysis of test results, particularly those of standardized tests. Such analyses can be very helpful as a means of addressing student problems as well as instructional weaknesses. Standardized tests are attractive as a beginning point because the test publishers routinely provide students' results in aggregate and disaggregated form to serve the needs of teachers and administrators.

Content areas in which the class as a whole or a subgroup of students (e.g., boys or girls) does not perform at a desired level can initiate self-evaluation. Analysis of data for a single class may identify several problem areas. Confirmation of the problem areas can be obtained by review across classes and years. Once a problem area is targeted, the teacher asks, "What is it about what I know or do (e.g., my knowledge or my skills in presentation) or in the instructional setting that could be changed to improve student learning?"

Thus, once a problem area is targeted, the teacher moves from the test results to analysis of his or her teaching program. Here, all aspects of the instruction can be considered. The teacher's knowledge and skill in teaching is part of the analysis issue, but the problem may also be due to other factors such as amount of time on the topic, curriculum coverage, poor quality of commercially available materials, or even lack of student effort.

This analysis of instruction can be either retrospective or prospective and routinely would include (a) a contingency analysis to determine whether the instruction as planned logically leads to the desired learning and (b) a congruence analysis to determine what actually occurs in instruction, whether it is consistent with plans, and whether and in what regard the desired objectives were achieved.

A retrospective analysis would use extant materials such as textbooks, lesson plans, amount of time devoted to instruction, samples of student work (homework and tests), instructional aids (e.g., transparencies), and practices and guides used in the instructional process. Because we know the strong tendency toward self-denial or self-protection, this analysis is probably best conducted with a partner who is knowledgeable about the content and teaching practices.

A prospective analysis would probably use many of the same materials as a retrospective analysis as well as some new ones, such as student reactions and classroom observations, but would occur in the context of current teaching efforts. As such, many self-evaluation activities would fit into the teacher's ongoing class preparation and delivery and thus probably would seem less like an add-on activity. However, the prospective strategy also carries some liabilities. If the areas to be addressed are identified a long time before the prospective evaluation occurs, problem context may be forgotten in the interim. The general content problem may be remembered, but the specific, initially identified weakness may be forgotten. Also, if the teacher's knowledge or the instructional strategy is poor, the prospective analysis will uncover the problem at the point when the topic or concept is to be taught or has just been taught, leaving little time to rectify personal knowledge or skill.

An advantage to this strategy is that targeted areas can be identified across teachers and grades to help integrate curricular and instructional strategies at the same time that opportunities are used for individual staff development. A second advantage is that group efforts can provide a collegial focus on self-evaluation and mutual reinforcement to carry through.

The strategy opens the door to student involvement both in analysis of the test data and in analysis of the learning situation. For example, several students who took the exam could be invited to participate in the identification of problem areas and in the analysis of the instructional approach used. Their inclusion provides an opportunity to develop a sense of a learning community with students (and perhaps with parents as well).

By carefully choosing the nature of test reports, the analytical skills needed by teachers can be kept to a minimum, and the attention of teachers can be quickly focused on identifying target areas of concern.

The process begins by using extant data. As such, self-evaluation begins with the interpretation of data rather than the gathering of data. That is probably a more interesting way to begin. The process provides an opportunity to apply a variety of strategies, because data can be brought to the issue from so many sources.

The process can be embedded in normal curriculum and classroom evaluation processes. As such, it more easily becomes an integral part of the teaching routine.

Incorporating a formal self-evaluation component into teacher self-evaluation can provide teachers with a sense of ownership of the evaluation, as well as genuine insight into and development of their own professional practice.

Example 19

Area Assessed: Practice

SELF-EVALUATION STRATEGY: TEACHER SELF-REFLECTION TOOL

The following statements describe possible standards and expectations teachers hold for students. Read each statement and circle the option that best describes your agreement or disagreement (SA = *strongly agree*; A = *agree*; U = *uncertain*; D = *disagree*; SD = *strongly disagree*). When finished, use the following page to help interpret your responses.

1. I have the same expectations for everyone.   SA   A   U   D   SD

2. There is a certain amount of work to be done in   SA   A   U   D   SD
   this course, and I expect everybody to do it.

3. I have different expectations for different kids.   SA   A   U   D   SD
   There are certain demands I just don't make on
   the lower-ability students.

4. I know some of them can't be expected to perform   SA   A   U   D   SD
   as well as others; it is this way in any large group.

5. I have different expectations for different kids.   SA   A   U   D   SD
   I know some of them have better backgrounds for
   getting this material and maybe they're just quicker.

6. I make special provisions for the slower students to   SA   A   U   D   SD
   try to bring them along as far and as fast as they can.

7. I understand that kids have different abilities and   SA   A   U   D   SD
   speeds of learning, but I also know what a quality
   performance from a student is like.

8. I press students toward a standard of excellence.   SA   A   U   D   SD
   I provide extra boosts and help those who need
   it, and I know they'll still move along at different
   rates and with different degrees of success. But the
   standard is still there, and I push them toward it.

Each of the previous statements corresponds to a particular perception of standards and their use in teaching. Decide which of the statements most closely reflect your beliefs about standards (i.e., with which statements you most strongly agree or disagree). The following chart defines various perceptions and uses of teaching standards.

Statement #	Type of teacher	Explanation
1 and 2	Nondiscriminating	Teacher does not make discriminations between students. Expectations are conceived in terms of coverage or amount of work completed rather than quality of performance.
3 and 4	Differential and accepting	Teacher forecasts that students have different abilities and will perform according to those abilities. Performances are accepted as representing what the students are capable of. All students get pretty much the same material, and they do what they can.
5 and 6	Differential and provisioning	Teacher forecasts that students have different abilities and will perform according to those abilities. Teacher provides for students who look like they'll have difficulty.
7 and 8	Image of excellence	A standard of excellence is held out for all students as a challenge and as a purpose for instruction. Teacher realizes that students have different capacities and different rates for learning, and he or she makes allowances by providing extra help to those who need it. Teacher never forgets the standard or lets students forget it.

SOURCE: Adapted from Saphier and Gower (1987).

What type of teacher are you when it comes to the use of teaching standards (i.e., nondiscriminating, differential and accepting, differential and provisioning, image of excellence)?

How does your perception and use of standards affect your teaching? Compare your responses to those obtained by giving a modified version of the reflection tool to pupils.

5 Developing Self-Evaluation Tools

Although this book provides some examples of formal self-evaluation approaches, it obviously is not possible to provide examples for every possible area in which teachers might want to self-evaluate. So, as teachers expand their self-evaluation activities beyond those we have provided, it will be necessary for them to develop their own instruments suitable to the areas of practice they wish to evaluate. This chapter offers suggestions for developing such self-evaluation tools.

When teaching performances, such as oral questioning, rule setting, and provision of feedback, or teacher products, such as lesson plans, tests, and grades, are evaluated, it is necessary to have a set of criteria to guide evaluation. These criteria identify the features that correspond to a good or desirable performance or product. Identifying such criteria is a critical part of the self-evaluation process, because they provide a focus for evidence gathering by pinpointing desired features of a performance or product that should be observed and evaluated. They provide the information that enables diagnosis of specific strengths and weaknesses associated with a teacher performance or product. Refer to Examples 2, 5, 6, 7, 8, 9, 10, 16, and 17 to see examples of criteria for examining a cooperative learning lesson, a teacher's feedback to students, classroom environment or climate, and general teaching performance. Without criteria such as these, the information obtained in self-evaluations will be unfocused and undiagnostic.

There are two primary sources from which criteria for self-evaluation can be derived: (a) a few selected teachers or all teachers in a grade or school collectively identifying important aspects of a performance or product and (b) using or modifying existing sets of criteria for a given performance or product. There are strengths and weaknesses to each approach, although each does lead to a set of usable criteria for self-evaluation.

Imagine a group of teachers who wished to evaluate their oral questioning strategies. To do this meaningfully, they must have some idea of the desirable and undesirable features of oral questioning. That is, they must decide on a set of criteria for evaluating oral questioning. A couple of nominated teachers or the group as a whole talks through the answer to the question "What makes for good oral questioning?" One teacher might suggest that they ought to call on a range of students. Another might suggest that there ought to be a mixture of higher- and lower-level questions. (Perhaps the teachers pause here to discuss the differences between higher- and lower-level questions.) Another teacher might suggest that questions ought to be worded clearly enough to be understood by all students, whereas a fourth might suggest that encouragement and follow-up questions should be given to pupils who give a partial or incomplete answer.

As teachers talk among themselves about the criteria of good oral questioning, a number of benefits ensue. First, the teachers are collaborating and interacting around a given problem. Second, they are sharing perceptions of good oral questioning strategies and undoubtedly learning from each other. Third, they are arriving at a common definition of good oral questioning, one that is likely to prevail in all their classes. Fourth, they are identifying the criteria that can be used to self-evaluate oral questioning. Fifth, the process is likely to help teachers to modify and improve their understanding of important concepts such as higher- and lower-level questions. Sixth, because a likely self-evaluation technique to gather information about a teacher's oral questioning is observation by a colleague, they are ensuring that their colleagues will have a common understanding of the desired criteria of good performance. The major disadvantage of teacher-generated criteria is the time it takes to arrive at a common and meaningful set of criteria through the group process.

Alternatively, teachers can seek out existing criteria for given teacher performances or products. A partial list of useful sources for criteria is provided at the end of this chapter. Textbooks focused on introduction to teaching methods or learning to teach also provide sets of criteria for most common teacher performances and products. Although it is not necessary to accept and adopt these criteria without modification, the benefit of using and modifying existing criteria is efficiency, insofar as selecting or adapting criteria takes less time than creating them from scratch. However, the collegial benefits that result from teachers working together are often lost in this approach.

Regardless of which approach is adopted, the following guidelines will help to identify and state useful criteria for self-evaluation.

1. There is no single best set of criteria for a given performance or product. Include those criteria that are both important and feasible in your

particular situation. There is always a trade-off between the quality of the information one collects and the ease of obtaining it. Feasibility should be an important consideration in defining criteria and collecting information about them.

2. It is appropriate to add to, eliminate, or modify existing criteria to align them to your needs.

3. For any given teacher performance or product, keep the evaluation criteria to a manageable number, usually not more than 10. Too many criteria make observation and evaluation difficult and inaccurate.

4. State criteria in terms of behaviors or features that can be observed and evaluated. Don't say, "Asks proper questions." Be specific and say instead, "Asks questions using age-appropriate vocabulary." Don't say, "Displays good feedback." Be specific and say instead, "Provides feedback relevant to the pupil's needs." Be precise and clear in stating the criteria so that an observer or judge will be left with minimum uncertainty about what should be observed. In general, avoid adverbs such as "good," "correct," and "appropriate," because they tend to obscure the specific performance of interest.

5. List the criteria on a sheet and have the sheet available when the performance or product is being evaluated. Maintain a written record, in terms of the criteria, when evaluating the performance or product.

6. Revise criteria as needed or as experience dictates.

Annotated Source List

The following sources provide useful suggestions and examples for defining self-evaluation criteria.

Angelo, T. A., & Cross. K. P. (1993). *Classroom assessment techniques* (2nd ed.). San Francisco: Jossey-Bass.

> Although geared to college teaching, this volume is one of the richest available collections of classroom assessment strategies, including self-evaluation. Detailed descriptions and examples are provided.

Arends, R. I. (1994). *Learning to teach* (2nd ed.). New York: McGraw.

> This introduction-to-teaching textbook covers many aspects of teaching knowledge and process and as such is a convenient source to identify areas for self-evaluation. The end-of-chapter exercises can be used as self-evaluation tools. Most introduction-to-teaching texts are useful sources for self-evaluation ideas.

Haysom, J. (1985). *Inquiring into the teaching process: Towards self-evaluation and professional development.* Research in education series (Vol. 12). Toronto: Ontario Institute for Studies in Education Press.

This book contains a number of strategies and examples of self-evaluation approaches.

Kremer-Hayon, L. (1993). *Teacher self-evaluation.* Boston: Kluwer Academic.

This book describes many approaches to teacher self-evaluation.

Pollard, A., & Tann, S. (1993). *Reflective teaching in the primary school* (2nd ed.). London: Cassell Educational Limited.

This text contains a large number of reflective and self-evaluation activities. Although aimed mainly at elementary grades, it also contains activities for all grade levels.

Rosenshine, B., & Stevens, R. (1986). Teaching functions. In M. C. Wittrock (Ed.), *Handbook of research on teaching* (3rd ed., pp. 376-391). New York: Macmillan.

This book describes the characteristics of many teacher performances and products.

Saphier, J., & Gower, R. (1987). *The skillful teacher.* Carlisle, MA: Research for Better Teaching.

An exceptionally thorough description of the knowledge base of teaching practice, with processes broken down into their essential elements. This book is a rich source of ideas and areas in which to carry out self-evaluations.

SouthEastern Regional Vision for Education (SERVE), School of Education, University of North Carolina at Greensboro, Greensboro, NC 27412.

SERVE has been working with schools in the Southeast on issues and practices of formative teacher self-evaluation.

6 Getting Started

Overcoming Barriers

In the first part of this chapter, we describe actions or conditions to help overcome barriers to individual teachers' starting the self-evaluation process. In the second section, we discuss broader schoolwide actions that can encourage the persistence and growth of self-evaluation. Both the individual and schoolwide conditions may seem commonsensical, but too often they are overlooked or ignored to the detriment of the self-evaluation process and teacher improvement. There are eight teacher-oriented activities that enhance the conduct of self-evaluation:

1. Volunteering
2. Focusing on awareness of practice
3. Starting small
4. Delimiting the focus of self-evaluation
5. Allocating time
6. Employing explicit criteria and standards
7. Making use of available resources
8. Learning about self-evaluation

Volunteering

The core objective of self-evaluation is self-improvement, something we all value. However, among those who have studied self-evaluation there is agreement that for meaningful change to occur, a teacher must be willing to participate and change. But despite our good intentions, we are not always willing or able to invest in either the process or the change dictated by self-evaluation. There are many reasons for this inability to follow through on improvement strategies. Some are tied to external forces (e.g., work expectations). Some are very personal in nature (e.g., simple inertia, habit, "I don't like being pushed into anything," and "That way may be better but it requires a lot more work"). Nonetheless, a core ingredient of any self-evaluation plan is "buy in" by a teacher or group of teachers. If you really want to use self-evaluation for personal improvement, you must willingly participate and engage in the process. Once you have chosen to engage, other issues become important.

Focusing on Awareness of Practice

Most of what we do in life is habitual. We talk, act, and teach doing many things that are so customary that we do not stop to think about them. Without being aware of one's practice, that is, understanding what one really believes, knows, and does in the classroom, it is difficult to change or improve.

Because self-evaluation focuses on personal improvement, a necessary beginning point is awareness of personal beliefs, knowledge, activities, and effectiveness. You can begin this clarification process quickly and easily by questioning one or two of your practices as you conduct your daily work. This self-examination process is simple and easily conducted, but it can have substantial ramifications for personal and self-evaluation actions to be taken. You might want to start with one of the strategies presented earlier.

Starting Small

Remember, the ultimate goal is development of long-term habits. To reach a habit stage with self-evaluation, one must not only begin the process but also appreciate and value it so that one continues self-evaluation for the long term. Begin with small self-evaluation activities that can be done easily. They will provide prompt rewards and will in themselves be satisfying. The suggested steps to follow are listed below:

Engage slowly. It makes little sense to start by engaging in a massive self-evaluation effort that will quickly wear you out and drain your enthusiasm. You would not start a marathon as though you were running a hundred-yard dash. Pick a narrow, "safe" area to begin your self-evaluation activities.

Identify strengths as well as weaknesses. Maintaining strong performances is as important as modifying poor ones. Besides, it is reinforcing and important to your sense of well-being to be reminded that you do some things well.

Take pride in undertaking your own professional development. Much of self-evaluation helps to uncover and change weaknesses, but change is never easy. Expect problems and, when they occur, draw strength from your willingness to engage in self-evaluation and the importance of improving to better serve your students.

As these guidelines suggest, when beginning self-evaluation don't try to change all parts of your beliefs and practices immediately. Begin with the expectation that by taking small, safe, regular steps toward self-improvement you will move in the correct direction.

Delimiting the Focus of Self-Evaluation

Be specific and narrow in your self-evaluation focus. Don't try to become aware of or change everything all at once. Instead, focus on one small issue at a time. The objective is self-improvement, and a good way to tackle this objective is to divide a larger area (e.g., instruction) into smaller pieces (e.g., planning, questioning, or setting expectations) that, when addressed, will result in incremental improvement.

Allocating Time

To reap the benefits of self-evaluation, it must be given some priority. This means that it must have its own designated time in the course of the day, even if that time is only 5 minutes. Try to keep it from being swallowed up by the mass of other issues and activities pressing for your attention. Planning for self-evaluation by building it into your schedule of activities and employing time-efficient exercises (e.g., the Minute Survey described in Example 3) can help you allocate time for self-evaluation.

Employing Explicit Criteria and Standards

As previously noted, self-evaluation, instruction, and learning are improved when care is taken to specify the criteria that will apply in examining a process or product and the standards that will be employed for determining success. Clear and specific criteria and standards focus attention on the important aspects of teaching activities, products, and outcomes. These are powerful reasons to employ criteria and standards in self-evaluation.

Making Use of Available Resources

Just because you are engaged in a self-improvement activity does not mean that you should exclude other people or resources from your self-evaluation. Frequently, other teachers, administrators, students, and aides will be interested and quite willing to help by providing materials, advice, and peer reviews. When such resources can serve your needs and perhaps benefit others as well, use them. However, be careful to decide beforehand whether the costs associated with use of other resources are likely to outweigh the benefits.

Learning About Self-Evaluation

You already know the excitement and increased interest that comes with learning new things. That is probably a major reason why you teach. Apply that lesson to yourself. There are many ways to use self-evaluation beneficially. Study of the topic will provide opportunities to modify and improve your own strategies and add to the variety of strategies employed. Ultimately, if you learn well and choose judiciously, you should find self-evaluation permeating much of your professional and personal life.

Building a Support Structure

Just as there are barriers that individual teachers must strive to overcome, the school context itself can either enhance or hinder the potential for successful teacher self-evaluation. Thus self-evaluation is heavily dependent on both teacher and principal or administrator commitment. A school-based support structure should provide for several important matters:

1. Awareness of self-evaluation and encouragement for teachers to conduct self-evaluation
2. Direct assistance to teachers in learning about self-evaluation
3. School policy that formally establishes self-evaluation as an integral part of the school structure
4. Guidelines that directly help teachers in their conduct of self-evaluation
5. Resources to help and encourage teacher self-evaluation processes
6. Safeguards to protect teachers

Awareness of Self-Evaluation and Encouragement for Teachers to Conduct Self-Evaluation

It is important that self-evaluation be brought to the attention of teachers and encouraged as a schoolwide practice. This is important because few teachers initiate and regularly use formal self-evaluation activities in their current school environments. Awareness and encouragement can be accomplished in many ways, including making written resource information available to teachers, discussing self-evaluation in meetings, and setting expectations for the conduct of self-evaluation.

The main objective of these activities is to create and sustain a positive environment for self-evaluation, one that supports self-evaluation interests, trust, and a general focus on the importance of professional development. Quite important to generating and sustaining this environment is administrator interest in and encouragement of teacher self-evaluation activities.

Direct Assistance to Teachers in Learning About Self-Evaluation

We know that most teachers have received little instruction in assessment and self-evaluation. Teachers can gain the information necessary to properly conduct self-evaluation through personal reading or inservice instruction geared to their needs. Once a group of teachers has experience in conducting self-evaluation, those teachers can help other teachers begin the process.

What should instruction provide? We think that at a first and basic level, instruction needs to provide awareness of self-evaluation options, opportunities, and pitfalls. At a second level, instruction can provide basic ideas and information for planning, organizing, and implementing self-evaluation in schools and classrooms. At a third level, instruction can directly address the four areas of self-evaluation implementation: delineating, obtaining data, reflecting and decision making, and applying decisions. Fourth and finally, instruction can directly address specific techniques, evidence gathering, and decision making about practice.

School Policy That Formally Establishes Self-Evaluation as an Integral Part of the School Structure

Few things are universally acclaimed and accepted from the outset. Most need time and opportunity to become established and formal recognition to ensure longevity. Providing for self-evaluation within school policy provides those assurances. Making self-evaluation an option within the formal structure of the school raises the relative importance of self-evaluation and enhances its long-term viability by setting expectations and assurances that self-evaluation is there to stay.

Guidelines That Directly Assist Teachers in Their Conduct of Self-Evaluation

Guidelines set out the general parameters for conducting self-evaluation in the school. Flowing from and operationalizing school policy guidelines can give self-evaluation the exposure, standing, and credibility needed to encourage teachers to employ self-evaluation in their classrooms. Importantly, schoolwide guidelines can ensure that self-evaluation activities obtain the requisite resources, are conducted as part of the normal expectations for professional development in the school, are conducted appropriately, and are integrated with other aspects of instruction and evaluation. See Resource C for one school's guidelines for self-evaluation.

For individual teachers, guidelines can help to ensure that the best strategies are employed and that the resulting self-evaluations are most advantageous for teachers. Finally, guidelines will help to ensure that self-evaluation meets the personnel evaluation standards for propriety, utility, feasibility, and accuracy; all are important to the long-term viability of self-evaluation within the school and classroom.

Resources to Help and Encourage Teacher Self-Evaluation Processes

A clear indicator of the importance of any initiative is the willingness of the school administrator to apply resources to it. Such resources can be money, provision of physical facilities, time, classroom aides, opportunity to visit with and learn from others, and a host of other possibilities. These resources are likely to be most beneficial to the development and maintenance of self-evaluation if directly included in the school's guidelines for self-evaluation. That way, all teachers will be aware of the options and opportunities available for self-evaluation activities.

We know that self-evaluation can lead to its own rewards of improved knowledge and skill. However, we also know that self-evaluation competes for time and attention against myriad other demands. If the school provides tangible benefits (e.g., resources and materials) in a fair and equitable way, such benefits are likely to serve as encouragement and reinforcement for conducting self-evaluation. What benefits the school chooses to bestow should be carefully prescribed within the constraints posed by the school's other programs and the conditions of contractual arrangements with teachers and administrators.

Safeguards to Protect Teachers

Ensure unbiased self-evaluation decisions. For self-evaluation to be useful, it must be based on unbiased information. Two main factors contribute to good self-evaluation decisions: valid information about practice and elimination or reduction of personal bias when interpreting information. Bias is reduced when self-evaluation is conducted in an environment of support and trust in which teachers can take an honest look at their practices without fear of sanction or penalty. Bias is also reduced when teachers learn to gather information that provides a basis for valid judgments about practice and when they obtain feedback from colleagues.

Protect teachers' rights and self-efficacy. Self-evaluation is inherently risky. It is never fun to learn that there are weaknesses in one's practice or that one's beliefs about instruction are not manifested in the classroom. Negative information can be seized by others and used to the detriment of the self-evaluating teacher. School policy should provide guidelines for protecting the rights and self-efficacy of teachers engaged in self-evaluation. Concrete commitments that ensure privacy of self-evaluation information and protect teachers who identify weaknesses in their practice must be provided at the school level.

Protect the voluntary nature of self-evaluation. Care needs to be taken to ensure the voluntary nature of self-evaluation. In particular, it is important to keep self-evaluation information and processes separate from externally imposed, summative evaluations. If voluntary and imposed teacher evaluations are mingled, teachers are likely to lose the feeling of volunteerism and the sense of personal empowerment that are fundamental to self-evaluation. (See Resource B for examples of schoolwide policies that address the safeguards discussed here.)

Ensure continued integrity of the system. Monitor the self-evaluation system to ensure that it continues to function with integrity across time. Many programs start well but change shape over time, inadvertently or purposely becoming weakened. To safeguard against such threats, school guidelines should provide for regular monitoring and review of the system.

Resource A
Teacher Self-Evaluation

Description of Formal Approaches

This section summarizes formal self-evaluation strategies that teachers can and do use. A common format is used to describe each of the strategies. This format has the following eight parts:

1. Name of approach
2. Distinctive features
3. Common variations
4. Purposes or uses
5. Performance criteria and standards
6. General timetable
7. Advantages
8. Disadvantages

The respective descriptions are intentionally brief, because the intent is to identify and overview each strategy. For examples of the following strategies, see Chapter 4.

Data Collection Method: Teacher Self-Reflection Tool

Distinctive Features

This tool is designed to be completed by the teacher, allowing him or her to evaluate his or her own performance in particular areas identified on the tool. This is usually a short, one- to two-page form containing a series of brief evaluation criteria or standards by which the teacher evaluates his or her own performance. Such an instrument is self-administered and self-analyzed.

Common Variations

The *checklist* is a series of statements or teaching goals used by the teacher to determine whether he or she exhibits that behavior, usually using a yes-no or a present-absent response. The *scaled instrument* is a series of statements or teaching goals by which the teacher rates his or her own performance, usually using a graduated response. The *questionnaire* is a series of open-ended questions to which the teacher responds in a narrative form.

Purposes or Uses

Because a self-reflection tool is self-administered and self-analyzed, the teacher is the sole provider of feedback. Thus this method is intended to spur the teacher's thinking, awareness, and self-reflection, rather than to provide objective feedback from external sources. These tools usually serve to focus the teacher's attention on specific teaching duties, goals, or standards and to evaluate his or her own performance in those areas. This would likely heighten a teacher's awareness of practice and perhaps lead to a "to do" list for teaching improvement.

Performance Criteria and Standards

The determination of performance criteria standards is an integral part of the self-evaluation process. When criteria and standards are used, they tend to be derived from one of four basic sources: research on effective teaching practices, theoretically based teaching models, author's judgments of what is appropriate, and individual teacher or school-based criteria.

General Timetable

It is advocated throughout the literature that self-evaluation practices should be engaged in on an ongoing, continuous basis. Teachers are encouraged to incorporate self-evaluation into their teaching routines by implementing practices throughout the school year rather than using a one-shot approach such as at the end of the year. Self-evaluation should be formative rather than summative. Self-evaluation is commonly referred to as a cyclical process in the literature, and teachers are urged to commit to it by allocating time and effort on a continual basis.

Advantages

1. Time efficient
2. Easily administered and analyzed
3. Inexpensive
4. Nonthreatening
5. No formal data analysis is required because responses indicate teacher judgment

Disadvantages

1. Standards for evaluation often are not specifically defined. That is, the teacher is rarely provided an external frame of reference to judge his or her own behavior.
2. This method requires that the teacher rely on memory and subjective responses. It is possible that teachers will have inaccurate self-perceptions, selective memory, or unreliable self-reflection.
3. Little specific guidance is provided for teaching improvement.

Data Collection Method: Media Recording and Analysis

Distinctive Features

The teacher uses media to record a sample of his or her own teaching in the classroom and subsequently analyzes it using an observation tool. Actual teaching behaviors are examined during analysis.

Common Variations

Common variations include the use of audiotape recordings and videotape recordings; an assistant may be present in the room to operate and monitor equipment or the teacher may operate the equipment himself or herself. Also, another person may be present during the analysis of the recording to serve as an observer and consultant. Variations on observation include expert-prepared, commercially available, and teacher-made instruments.

Microteaching is often used during preservice training. The process generally entails students' receiving instruction on particular teaching skills, such as wait time for questioning or higher-level questioning, and then practicing those behaviors by teaching a group of five to six other preservice teachers for 10-20 minutes. The mock teaching session is videotaped and later observed by the instructor and the student. An observation instrument is used to guide analysis and evaluation of the specific teaching behaviors.

Purposes or Uses

Media recording is intended to provide the teacher with a concrete, stable documentation of teaching performance. This can be viewed and analyzed shortly after recording. It can also be archived for future use, such as comparison with future performance. The observation tool is intended to focus analysis on evaluation criteria. It serves as a data-gathering device to document specific teaching behaviors and their frequency.

Performance Criteria and Standards

Analysis of the recording is usually guided by use of an observation tool that identifies criteria to be used in analyzing the recording. Like self-reflection tools, criteria may come from research on teaching effectiveness, the literature, commercial instruments, or instruments self-made by the teacher or school district. A teacher may also decide to review the recording without the guidance of an observation tool, thereby observing performance without the guidance of predetermined evaluation criteria.

Media recording is most suitable for observation of particular teaching behaviors and mannerisms, such as tone of voice, body language, facial expressions, and movement throughout the classroom, as opposed to student achievement. It can, however, be used to record student behaviors and observe activity around the classroom that may be missed while involved in the teaching act.

Criteria are usually determined prior to recording and analysis by choosing or developing an observation tool. Teaching goals or criteria that are specific and defined in behavioral terms simplify data collection during the analysis phase. Desired behaviors must be identified so they can be recognized or missed during viewing. The observation tool provides a system for coding behavior.

General Timetable

See Teacher Self-Reflection Tool section.

Advantages

1. This method is more systematic than self-reflection tools. It allows more objectivity because it doesn't require the teacher to rely on memory to recall teaching performance.

2. The recording may be replayed as often as needed for careful analysis and saved for future analysis and comparison with other recordings.

3. The teacher does not have to depend on an external observer to view teaching unless he or she chooses to employ someone to view the recording and provide feedback.

4. The method can be nonthreatening because the teacher may view the recording privately if he or she chooses.

5. The teacher can determine the length of recording time or how often the method is employed.

6. If students are aware that their teacher cares to evaluate his or her own performance and make improvements, this sends a powerful message to students that the teacher places a high priority on effective teaching.

Disadvantages

1. The process is time-consuming because it requires that the teacher obtain equipment and arrange for or perform setup and tear down. In addition, analysis of the event may take as long or longer than the recorded event itself.

2. It requires planning and added expenditure of effort on the part of the teacher and any assistants or consultants he or she may employ.

3. It can cause disruption or distraction during class time, especially when students are not accustomed to being recorded. This can have an artificial effect on classroom interactions until the novelty diminishes.

4. Although the recording is meant to provide an objective document of actual teaching behavior, the analysis can still be subject to the biases of the observers. Research shows this method is most effective with secure, self-confident people, if the taped individual is the only participant in playback analysis.

5. This method is appropriate for evaluating only certain teaching competencies such as behaviors that are readily observable during classroom instruction. For example, it lends itself to evaluation of verbal and nonverbal interaction but is not the best choice of techniques to evaluate grading practices or test-item construction.

6. There is an absence of research on the effectiveness of media recording and analysis.

7. Research shows that although media recording devices are widely available to teachers, they are used minimally.

8. Limitations in the pickup device (camera, microphone, etc.) can cause distortions in both sound and picture quality and in context of the whole classroom environment.

Data Collection Method: Student Feedback Tool

Distinctive Features

This tool is similar to the self-reflection tool except that students complete the form instead of the teacher.

Common Variations

As with the teacher self-reflection tool, student feedback tools can be checklists, scaled instruments, or open-ended questionnaires. Students may also be asked to complete a form about specific classroom events or teacher behaviors, providing the teacher with information about student perceptions. For example, students may provide information about a specific teaching behavior that the teacher wishes to examine in his or her normal teaching pattern, such as the use of praise or wait time after asking questions. Feedback tools may also be used to obtain the perceptions of other external sources, such as peers, parents, and supervisors. Teachers may also complete the tool. They may predict students' responses and then compare them to actual responses. They may also use the tool to rate themselves and compare self-perceptions to student ratings. Areas of possible improvement can be determined from the discrepancies. Student feedback tools serve to bridge the gap between teachers' self-perceptions and the perceptions of significant others, usually students. A less formal variation of obtaining student feedback is through direct conversation with students.

Purposes or Uses

This method allows the teacher to learn students' perceptions of teaching behavior. It facilitates feedback from a more objective source than self-reflection and requires that teachers bridge the gap between self-perceptions and students' assessment of performance. If teacher self-perceptions are incongruent with student perceptions, the teacher has this information and can address discrepancies.

Performance Criteria and Standards

The evaluation standards for student feedback tools are determined as they are for teacher self-reflection tools. In this case, however, students may also have input as to requirements for effective teaching when they respond to open-ended comment sections. For example, they may choose to address an area not specifically defined on the tool. As with teacher self-reflection tools, the performance criteria may be specifically defined for students, or it may be left to the students discretion. For example, a desired length of wait time after the teacher asks a question may be provided, and the student is asked if the teacher meets that standard. On the other hand, the student may merely be asked if the teacher waits long enough after asking questions. Thus, the student is left to decide what is appropriate.

General Timetable

See Teacher Self-Reflection Tool section.

Advantages

1. Research demonstrates that students can provide valid feedback about the quality of instruction they have received.
2. Research shows that teachers do change their teaching as a result of student feedback that is perceived as valid.
3. Research also shows that student ratings that are significantly lower than self-ratings will more likely lead to improvement.
4. Because students are most directly affected by instruction, the process empowers the students to influence their own instruction and makes them feel respected as valued participants in the teaching-learning process.

Disadvantages

1. This method can be threatening to teachers who fear feedback from students.
2. Students may mistrust the teacher's intentions and be apprehensive about responding truthfully.
3. Students may choose not to take the process seriously.
4. Students may need to be taught to be careful observers of the effect that teaching has on their learning. They must be tuned in to their own learning needs to perceive how different teaching behaviors influence their success.

Data Collection Method: Teacher Portfolio

Distinctive Features

A teaching portfolio is a collection of information that provides evidence about a teacher's effectiveness. In short, the teacher documents teaching successes or techniques by collecting and compiling representative samples of teaching performance along with written annotations and analyses. They can be longitudinal, similar to a scrapbook or dossier.

Common Variations

The portfolio can be structured around key dimensions of teaching, such as planning and preparation; student evaluation; professional development; and interactions with students, parents, or other teachers. A variety of evidence may go into a portfolio: student work; unit plans; student evaluations; professional publications; videotapes of teaching; samples of teaching materials; diagrams of classroom arrangements; evidence of help given to colleagues; information from others, such as observation of teaching by qualified others; and letters from students and parents. All this is accompanied by annotations from the teacher about his or her development and use. Portfolios can contain information gathered by the teacher, jointly by the teacher with others, or mainly by others. Portfolios might contain descriptions of classroom learning activities or examples of handouts, assignments, and tests. Actual samples of students work, feedback from students, letters from parents, snapshots of bulletin boards, and the like might also be included.

Purposes or Uses

The portfolio seeks to give evidence of performance in varied and changing conditions. Portfolios can be used for formative evaluation, thus serving the purpose of improvement only. Portfolios can be used to influence formal, summative evaluation decisions. When used during the traditional performance or merit evaluation process, it allows the teacher to provide input to the evaluator regarding teaching successes, student progress, or achievement of goals. Portfolios can be used to provide students with information about courses. The portfolio will serve as a reference for the teacher regarding previous teaching performance.

Performance Criteria and Standards

Evaluation of portfolio contents depends on professional judgment and is most successful when there are a few clear performance criteria. Research shows that portfolios must be used in conjunction with goal setting and planning to be beneficial. See Teacher Self-Reflection Tool section.

General Timetable

See Teacher Self-Reflection Tool section.

Advantages

1. When prepared for self-reflection and improvement purposes, it provides the teacher with a concrete record of selected, significant events. The process can be rewarding and would not necessarily be time-consuming.

2. When prepared as a part of the formal evaluation process, it provides the teacher with a chance to have input into his or her own evaluation.

3. A portfolio shows breadth of information about practice.

Disadvantages

1. When teaching goals or standards are not determined, the result could be unfocused and haphazard. The materials included could also be idiosyncratic and biased, because the teacher has a vested interest in

his or her own success. This is especially true when the contents are to be used for formal evaluation.

2. This method is time-consuming for the teacher and the assessor.

3. It is difficult to keep portfolio information secure.

Data Collection Method:
Student Performance Data

Distinctive Features

The teacher gathers and uses written documentation of student performance or behavior to analyze the effect of teaching on students' success or failure. The teacher begins by determining what a successful outcome would be. He or she then decides what kind of data to collect or use and when and how it will be collected. The feedback is used to inform teachers about student achievement, interests, attitudes, and the like and ultimately to guide teaching practices or emphasis. In short, the teacher determines criteria for desired behavior or learning outcomes and then uses student performance data to determine the achievement of those and the areas that need further attention.

Common Variations

The teacher can devise a simple tool to collect desired data. This can be a multiple-choice, scaled-response, or open-ended questionnaire. Such classroom assessment activities are differentiated from usual assignments and tests because they occur before students are evaluated on their learning, while there is still time to alter teaching and thus learning. The teacher may also use regular student assignments, quizzes, or tests to assess students' understanding of content.

For example, the number of student mistakes on a homework assignment can be tallied. The data can be analyzed for problems or successes in particular areas. Based on this information, the teacher can decide whether to reteach, modify future instruction, or move on to new content. The teacher may also create a written record of particular events to track student behaviors. An example of this would be if a teacher were to systematically record a particular student behavior, such as time-on-task during class, to be used for later analysis. Students may also be asked to chart their own behavior. Student dialogue and oral responses to questions can be charted and analyzed. This type of data collection and analysis is often done informally.

A technique known as action research echoes the student performance data use process. A teacher determines instructional objectives that are observable, measurable, and limited in number. A pretest is administered to measure these objectives. After the unit is taught, a posttest is administered. Students or teachers analyze the data and determine what teacher-controlled factors contributed to student success or nonsuccess. As a result, instructional strategies are developed to improve teaching and student learning. A teacher can decide to gather and analyze data regarding the whole class, small groups, or individuals.

Purposes or Uses

A review of student performance data may provide the initial needs assessment to identify areas where change or improvement is needed in teaching. For example, analysis of test responses can provide teachers with information regarding students' content knowledge. When weaknesses are uncovered, further instructional efforts may be undertaken. This method is used when a specific area has been targeted for analysis. The teacher is systematically gathering and using objective data to inform future teaching decisions. Evidence of student performance and behavior is used to guide the teacher's instruction as, for example, when test responses are used to determine students weaknesses in content knowledge.

Performance Criteria and Standards

Desired performance or behavior on the part of students is determined by the teacher prior to the collection of data. Criteria are often driven by content when student understanding is assessed. Content or curriculum standards are most often driven by the school or district. Particular student behaviors, such as arriving at class on time or being nondisruptive to other class members, may also be tracked and analyzed. These are often determined by the teacher but may also be guided by school or district standards. See Teacher Self-Reflection Tool section.

General Timetable

Classroom assessment techniques would ideally occur during each unit prior to testing. Use of assignments and tests would ideally occur as each is administered. Event recording would likely occur on an episodic or as-needed basis. See Teacher Self-Reflection Tool section.

Advantages

1. The use of concrete, objective data removes much of the bias that is associated with self-reflective methods. It focuses attention on student performance or behaviors.

2. Data can be efficiently and easily collected. When time-efficient classroom assessment activities are not used, teachers can use classroom assignments, quizzes, and tests because these are usually administered as a part of the normal routine anyway.

Disadvantages

1. Using student performance data is not traditionally viewed as a self-evaluation technique. Often, the focus is on student accountability and grading and not on diagnosing mastery and guiding teaching. As a result, such data are often undervalued and underused.

2. Teachers may avoid this method because it requires use of performance data for more than evaluation of students, and follow-through is necessary when data collected warrant reteaching of subject matter. Unlike some other methods, a teacher is less able to provide only favorable feedback.

3. Teachers may become bogged down in a plethora of student performance data unless strategies are employed to efficiently gather, select, manage, and analyze data.

4. Classroom assessment tools, assignments, and tests must be carefully designed to elicit students' mastery of content or desired outcomes. A poorly designed tool will not provide valuable data.

5. Teachers may require specific training to become skillful in using student performance data.

6. Little research has been done on the effect of student performance feedback on improvement of instruction.

Data Collection Method: External Observation

Distinctive Features

Teacher engages a colleague to observe teaching performance and provide feedback. Joint collaboration regarding desired teaching behaviors characterizes the process. This method is often used in conjunction with an observation tool to guide observation and analysis.

Common Variations

This method is often associated with formal teacher evaluation where the principal or supervisor uses classroom observation as part of the summative evaluation process. This method may also be quite informal such as when the teacher asks a colleague to observe for improvement only. In this case, formal evaluation standards may or may not be agreed on. Collaboration may occur with a peer, such as another teacher, a supervisor, or an instructional improvement specialist. The literature often advocates engaging in pre- and postconferences as a part of this process. During these conferences, the teacher and observer determine observation and evaluation criteria, discuss findings, engage in joint problem solving, and develop improvement plans.

External observation is commonly used during clinical supervision of preservice teachers. It is used for the purposes of improvement and summative evaluation. As in microteaching (see Media Recording and Analysis section), preservice teachers can practice new teaching behaviors or methods on each other and receive feedback from others regarding their effectiveness before employing the techniques in the classroom.

Purposes or Uses

This method provides another perspective to the teacher regarding his or her teaching performance. An observer can provide more objective feedback than the teacher can gather from reflection alone. It bridges the gap between personal perception, which may be biased, and the perceptions of others. The observer serves as the teacher's mirror, participating in mutual problem solving and providing recommendations for improvement.

Performance Criteria and Standards

These would be mutually determined between the teacher and his or her colleague. They may be guided by personal, school, or district goals, as well as the literature on teaching practice. For success in this process, criteria must be directly observable. See Teacher Self-Reflection Tool section.

General Timetable

This would be determined by the teacher and his or her colleague. See Teacher Self-Reflection Tool section.

Advantages

1. This method provides feedback that is more objective than a teacher's own perceptions. A teacher can benefit from another teaching professional's knowledge and feedback. The involvement of an external observer makes it less likely that the teacher could explain away or rationalize ineffective teaching behaviors.

2. Collegial dialogue and support can lessen feelings of isolation and frustration and increase the teacher's self-esteem. It can provide motivation and support to improve teaching and promote an atmosphere of collegiality. The teacher may benefit from the experiential wisdom of another teaching professional.

3. Minimal risk to the teacher is perceived when the technique is self-initiated. It is less threatening than formal performance evaluation by a supervisor.

4. Collecting data based on others' perceptions is advocated in the literature, because using more than one source of information decreases the possibility of personal misperception and provides a more thorough perspective of teaching performance.

Disadvantages

1. This method is time-consuming for both the teacher and his or her colleague. It requires a great deal of trust, so teachers may be reluctant to risk trying this method.

2. Some artificiality is introduced into the classroom experience. The presence of an outsider initially diverts attention and may create stress on the part of the teacher and curiosity among students.

3. This method may often be done among friends. Thus the process may benefit from the trusting relationship but may also suffer as a result of bias and lack of total honesty. Clear and candid, yet constructive, communication is essential to the process.

4. Observers must possess the necessary skills and expertise to provide valuable input to the teacher.

5. There is little research on the effects of this method on teaching improvement.

Data Collection Method: Journaling

Distinctive Features

The teacher uses a personal journal or written record to document significant events or outcomes and record and organize subsequent perceptions or findings.

Common Variations

Personal journals may be maintained to record teaching goals and document their progression. The journal may include documentation of significant events or interactions with students along with the teacher's ideas regarding the connotations that contributed to the success or failure of those events. Often, this method is reflective in nature. A written analysis of work can be maintained to document daily lesson plans and actual outcomes. For example, a lesson plan analysis can be used to document the success or shortcomings of lesson activities, hypothesize reasons for actual outcomes, and document improvement strategies. Records can also be indexed by problem or outcome, which may permit an analysis of common themes found under specific conditions.

Purposes or Uses

This method provides the teacher with a formal, written record of his or her own work and thought. When maintained over time, a journal serves as a database and provides both historical perspective and information about patterns of teacher behavior and thought.

Performance Criteria and Standards

Standards for judging the contents of a journal are rarely stated at the outset of journal preparation. Rather, they are implied within the context of the journal contents. In the case of indexing and documenting according to particular concerns, the standards may be more specifically defined. See Teacher Self-Reflection Tool section.

General Timetable

See Teacher Self-Reflection Tool section.

Advantages

1. The act of maintaining and reviewing a personal journal can serve as a therapeutic tool for teachers over time. It provides a window on the past and a record of growth.
2. Maintaining a systematic database of events can provide valuable data regarding trends and cause-and-effect patterns.
3. A journal can improve reflections by increasing their accuracy.

Disadvantages

1. Journaling is not delineated explicitly in the literature; rather, it is simply referred to as a desirable activity.
2. Journals are often reflective in nature and unsystematic. The contents included are a result of the teacher's particular interests, concerns, or biases.

Data Collection Method:
Collegial Dialogue and Problem Solving

Distinctive Features

Collaboration with other teaching professionals enables teachers to compare perceptions, share techniques, and jointly solve problems. Collegial dialogue may come about as a result of prior self-evaluation activities that may identify issues a teacher may want to talk through with colleagues. It may also be a teacher's main method of self-evaluation.

Common Variations

Teachers may participate in formal large- or small-group interactions during inservices or staff meetings. Such group interactions also often occur informally during lunch, in the teachers' lounge, or before and after school. Interaction may occur one-on-one or in small groups. Interaction may be planned or unplanned and spontaneous. The in-depth interview is another variation in which the teacher responds to probing questions that serve to enlighten and sensitize the teacher to his or her own teaching practices.

Purposes or Uses

This method provides the teacher with another point of view besides his or her own. The teacher can benefit from sharing his or her own experiences and gaining someone else's experience and insight.

Performance Criteria and Standards

These are most likely determined by the teacher as evidenced by the topic chosen for discussion. Current problems in the classroom are likely to trigger conversation. Teaching goals may also be guided by the school or district when discussion occurs as part of a formal inservice education activity. See Teacher Self-Reflection Tool section.

General Timetable

This is the type of self-evaluation activity that likely occurs frequently, both formally and informally. See also Teacher Self-Reflection Tool section.

Advantages

1. Teachers can benefit from their own local pool of knowledge—they are their own experts. Teachers become empowered problem solvers.
2. Isolation is decreased. A supportive environment and helping relationships are engendered, which increase self-esteem.
3. Research shows improvement in teaching practice as a result of engaging in dialogue with other teachers.

Disadvantages

1. The literature does not delineate a system for this process. It only refers to it as a desired outcome of self-evaluation. The method is not systematic.

2. Time constraints during the teaching day often preclude teachers from engaging in this activity. Current school cultures may not encourage exchange between teaching professionals.

Resource B
Self-Evaluation
Planning Resources

SERVE has worked with several schools in the design of a formative system. The list of questions below arose as the design teams applied the concept of a formative teacher evaluation system to their particular schools. Thus, a first step in beginning to think about a formative system for your school might be to discuss these questions as part of a planning group.

1. Who should be involved in designing the formative evaluation system?

   (Note: Although an administrator could design the system for teachers, this arrangement would likely generate less commitment on the part of teachers than a system designed and "owned" by the teachers and administrators.)

2. Who will participate in the formative system? Beginning teachers? Probationary teachers? Career status/tenured teachers?

3. Will participation on the formative system be voluntary? (Must volunteering teachers be approved by the administrator to go on a formative system? Should the criteria for approval be made explicit or left to the judgment of the school principal?)

4. What evaluation methods will be required of teachers on the formative system?
   a. Will only one method be specified (e.g., videotape review by peer), or will teachers choose several from a menu of methods?
   b. If peer review is involved, will there be a specified number of times feedback must be provided?

5. How and when will the formative process be reported to an administrator?
   a. Will there be a conference at the beginning and end of the year between each teacher and an administrator to discuss the teacher's formative plans?
   b. Will any paperwork be required for those on the formative system?
   c. How important is it for teachers to control the amount of information about their professional growth that is shared with an administrator?

6. What roles will the administrator play (e.g., selling the idea of formative evaluation to critics outside the school, facilitating resources and meetings, providing support and leadership that encourages risk taking without fear of failing, responding to teacher requests for assistance)?

7. What kinds of resources or support might be needed (e.g., videotapes, release time to observe others, and information on new practices)?

8. What kinds of training in peer conferencing and evaluation methods will be needed by participating teachers?

9. Will a review of the formative system be conducted by its designers to identify and solve any problems?

10. Will a review be conducted at the conclusion of the initial or pilot phase of the project to provide information about the formative system to external audiences, including the school board? (McColskey & Egelson, 1993)

For questions to ask in getting started with a schoolwide self-evaluation system, contact SouthEastern Regional Vision for Education (SERVE), School of Education, University of North Carolina at Greensboro, Greensboro, NC 27412.

Proposed Alternative Teacher Assessment
- **3-year program**
- **Tenured teachers**
- **Voluntary**

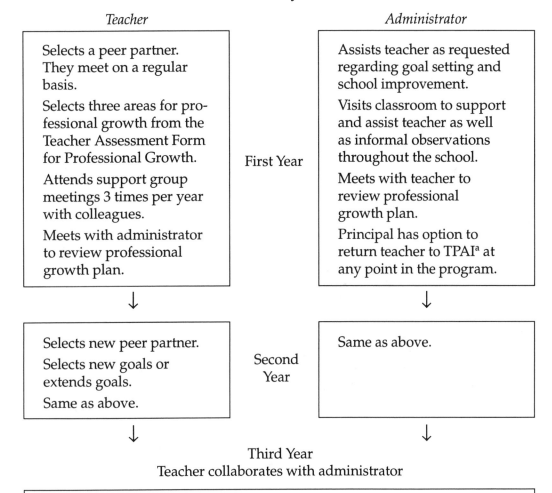

	Teacher		*Administrator*
	Selects a peer partner. They meet on a regular basis. Selects three areas for professional growth from the Teacher Assessment Form for Professional Growth. Attends support group meetings 3 times per year with colleagues. Meets with administrator to review professional growth plan.	First Year	Assists teacher as requested regarding goal setting and school improvement. Visits classroom to support and assist teacher as well as informal observations throughout the school. Meets with teacher to review professional growth plan. Principal has option to return teacher to TPAI[a] at any point in the program.
	↓		↓
	Selects new peer partner. Selects new goals or extends goals. Same as above.	Second Year	Same as above.
	↓		↓

Third Year
Teacher collaborates with administrator

Meet to set school, administration, and instructional/student goals (first collaborative meeting at end of second year).

Discuss and implement portfolio that reflects teacher's goals and principal's classroom visits.

Meet to discuss progress; any needed assistance (midyear meeting).

At end of year, meet to discuss portfolio, collaborate on future goals, directions, and visions of professional growth.

a. Teacher Performance Appraisal Instrument.
SOURCE: *The Guilford Plan: Alternative Teacher Assessment, a Dual Purpose System* (1992). Guilford County Schools, Greensboro, North Carolina. Reproduced by permission.

Figure B1.

Guilford County School System: Teacher Assessment Form for Professional Growth

Name: _____

School: _____ Certification: _____ Position/subject area: _____

School year: _____ Peer partner: _____

Evaluation methods chosen:

(Teacher must choose three methods to use at least once during the school year. One method must be chosen from the Peer Review category.)

Self

_____ Videotape of teaching
_____ Self-rating form (required)
_____ Journal
_____ Self-study materials
_____ Observation/modeling of
        another teacher
_____ Portfolio

_____ Development and presentation
        of content topics

Peer Review

_____ In-class observation by peers
_____ Videotape observation by peer
_____ Review by peer of journal

Student or Parent Feedback

_____ Student surveys or interviews
_____ Parent surveys or interviews

_____ Assessing student progress

Focus areas for peer review:

_____ Teaching behaviors and
        use of instructional methods
        (discipline, higher-level
        questioning, praise, coopera-
        tive learning)

Teacher's summary statement about professional development:

_____   _____   _____   _____
Teacher's signature   Date   Principal's signature   Date

SOURCE: *The Guilford Plan: Alternative Teacher Assessment, a Dual Purpose System* (1992). Guilford County Schools, Greensboro, North Carolina. Reproduced by permission.

Figure B2.

76

Resource C
Guilford County Formative
Teacher Evaluation Plan:
Questions and Answers

Q: Why did two schools in Guilford County develop a formative teacher evaluation plan?

A: Career teachers felt that the state teacher evaluation instrument (TPAS) addressed only a portion of teaching experience through the formal observation process and failed to promote teacher growth. Administrators were concerned about the inefficiency of annually evaluating teachers who had already proven themselves competent.

Q: How was the formative plan developed?

A: After SERVE training, the development team met regularly during the 1991-1992 school year. The group believed that the evaluation plan should include a variety of formative methods. The group spent several months developing the plan and then formulated strategies to publicize it. The team planned a 4-hour training session for interested teachers in May 1992.

Q: What are the characteristics of Guilford County's formative plan?

A: Participation is voluntary. Only tenured teachers are allowed to substitute a peer evaluation for traditional summative evaluation.

To participate, teachers must attend a training session on formative and summative teacher evaluations, formative evaluation methods, and basic conferencing skills.

Teachers select a peer partner for the year.

Teachers must choose two formative evaluation methods in addition to a required self-evaluation assessment. The two methods are selected from the following options: videotaping a lesson, keeping a journal or portfolio, observing exemplary teaching, being observed by a peer, completing self-study materials, and surveying parents or students. At least one of the two selected methods must involve a peer.

Paperwork is minimal. One form, submitted to the principal at the beginning of the year, indicates the three formative methods the teacher plans to use for the year. The other form, due at the end of the school year, requires the teacher's signature stating he or she has completed the requirements of the plan.

The pilot project is scheduled for 3 years. For 2 years, teachers are on the formative plan; the third year they are evaluated by a building administrator.

Teachers initiate a discussion with the school principal at the beginning and end of the school year about the evaluation methods they have chosen and their progress in implementing them. The teachers determine how much information about growth to share with the principal. The purpose is to keep the administrator informed.

Teachers participating in the formative plan who do not fulfill their professional responsibilities can be placed back on the summative system by their building administrator.

Teachers attend three support meetings during the year to share experiences and ideas.

Q: How did the team gain approval for the plan?

A: The development team presented the formative plan to district administrators in the spring of 1992. District administrators gave their approval for Guilford Middle School and Pleasant Garden Elementary School to participate in the 3-year pilot beginning in the fall of 1992.

Q: How many teachers are involved?

A: During the 1992-1993 school year, 70 tenured teachers from Guilford Middle School and Pleasant Garden Elementary School participated in the pilot.

Q: What problems did the development team experience, and how were they resolved?

A: At one school, teachers had difficulty finding time to implement the peer review associated with the plan because many of them were involved with other projects. The development team offered suggestions on how to find time to complete the peer evaluations (e.g., videotaping the classroom lessons and having the peer view them at home). Some teachers were initially unclear about what was expected of them, probably due to the fact that the evaluation plan was so different from what they were accustomed to and that several methods were allowed. The support group meetings provided an opportunity for the development team to review program guidelines with participating teachers.

Q: How have teachers and administrators reacted to the new plan?

A: Teachers like the freedom to select their own area of professional growth. They are particularly enthusiastic about the peer component of the plan. Administrators believe the formative model meets the needs of tenured teachers better than annual summative evaluations.

Q: What is the future of Guilford County's formative teacher evaluation plan?

A: Guilford County Schools merged with two other school systems in July 1993. The merged system has a new superintendent and a new school board. At this writing, Guilford Middle School and Pleasant Garden Elementary School teachers who have selected the formative plan as an option are in their second year of a 3-year pilot. The second-year plan is like the first except that the teachers select new peer partners, goals, and formative methods. In the third year of the plan, each teacher will meet with the building administrator to develop administrator, school, and instructional goals. Each teacher will keep a portfolio that reflects the goals he or she is working on for the year.

The formative teacher evaluation plan has been a good idea. Videotaping [a teacher conducting a lesson] can become a nonthreatening tool for improvement. Working with a peer partner is helpful because we really talk about teaching as opposed to the cursory discussions with administrators at postevaluation conferences.

Conclusions

At the close of the 1992-1993 school year, administrators and teachers in the three school systems where formative teacher evaluation plans were initiated reported

- Greater collegiality among faculty members
- An increased sense of professionalism among teachers
- A willingness on the part of teachers to discuss and improve weaknesses
- Improved classroom instruction

Members of the Formative Teacher Evaluation Plan Development Team for Guilford County Schools, Greensboro, North Carolina, were Judy Glasgow, Gloria Hatfield, Barbara Lambert, Linda Lindley, Patty MacMurray, and Liz Wakelin. For more information on this project, contact Barbara Lambert, Assistant Principal, Southwest Middle School, 4368 Barrow Road, High Point, NC 27265; (919) 454-4315.

Teachers and administrators who are interested in pursuing a partnership with SERVE for the purpose of developing a formative teacher evaluation plan in their schools should call SERVE at (800) 755-3277.

References

Airasian, P. W., & Gullickson, A. (1994). Examination of teacher self-assessment. *Journal of Personnel Evaluation in Education, 8*, 195-203.

Airasian, P. W., Gullickson, A., Hahn, L., & Farland, D. (1995). *Teachers' self-assessment: The literature in perspective.* Report submitted to the Office of Research, Office of Educational Research and Improvement, U.S. Department of Education, Washington, DC.

Angelo, T. A., & Cross, K. P. (1993). *Classroom assessment technique: A handbook for college teachers.* San Francisco: Jossey-Bass.

Clandinin, D. J., & Connelly, F. M. (1988). Studying teachers' knowledge of classrooms: Collaborative research, ethics, and the negotiation of narrative. *Journal of Educational Thought, 22*(2A), 269-282.

Gitlin, A., Bringhurst, K., Burns, M., Cooley, V., Myers, B., Price, K., Russell, R., & Tiess, P. (1992). *Teachers' voices for school change.* New York: Teachers College Press.

Gullickson, A., Airasian, P. W., & Assaff, E. (1994). Self-assessment "tool kit" designed to help teachers analyze practice. *CREATE Evaluation Perspectives 4*(3), pp. 1, 6-8.

Kremer-Hayon, L. (1993). *Teacher self-evaluation: Teachers in their own mirrors.* Boston: Kluwer Academic.

Kuhn, D. (1991). *The skill of argument.* New York: Cambridge University Press.

Little, J. W. (1993). Teachers' professional development in a climate of educational reform. *Educational Evaluation and Policy Analysis, 15*(2), 129-151.

McColskey, W., & Egelson, P. (1993). *Designing teacher evaluation systems that support professional growth*. Greensboro: University of North Carolina at Greensboro, SouthEastern Regional Vision for Education.

Nisbett, R. E., & Ross, L. (1980). *Human inference: Strategies and shortcomings of social judgment*. Englewood Cliffs, NJ: Prentice Hall.

Osterman, K. F., & Kottkamp, R. B. (1993). *Reflective practice for educators: Improving schooling through professional development*. Newbury Park, CA: Corwin.

Saphier, J., & Gower, R. (1987). *The skillful teacher*. Carlisle, MA: Research for Better Teaching.

Schon, D. A. (1983). *The reflective practitioner: How professionals think in action*. New York: Basic Books.

Stufflebeam, D. L., & Shinkfield, A. J. (1985). *Systematic evaluation*. Boston: Kluwer-Nijhoff.

CORWIN
PRESS

The Corwin Press logo—a raven striding across an open book—represents the happy union of courage and learning. We are a professional-level publisher of books and journals for K–12 educators, and we are committed to creating and providing resources that embody these qualities. Corwin's motto is "Success for All Learners."